Make Your Own

# JIGS & WOODSHOP FURNITURE

Make Your Own
# JIGS & WOODSHOP
# FURNITURE

## JEFF GREEF

BETTERWAY BOOKS

Cincinnati, Ohio

Make Your Own Jigs and Woodshop Furniture. Copyright © 1994 by Jeff Greef. Printed and bound in China. All rights reserved. No part of this book may be reproduced in any form or by any electronic or mechanical means including information storage and retrieval systems without permission in writing from the publisher, except by a reviewer, who may quote brief passages in a review. Published by Betterway Books, an imprint of F&W Publications, Inc., 1507 Dana Avenue, Cincinnati, Ohio, 45207. 1-800-289-0963. First edition.

This hardcover edition of *Make Your Own Jigs and Woodshop Furniture* features a "self-jacket" that eliminates the need for a separate dust jacket. It provides sturdy protection for your book while it saves paper, trees, and energy.

98    97    96    95    94        5    4    3    2    1

Library of Congress Cataloging in Publication Data

Greef, Jeff
    Make your own jigs and woodshop furniture / by Jeef Greef. — 1st ed.
        p.   cm.
    Includes index.
    ISBN 1-55870-340-3
    1. Woodworking tools. 2. Jigs and fixtures. 3. Workshops — equipment and supplies.  I. Title.
TT186.G74 1994
684'.08—dc20                                94-14764
                                                 CIP

Edited by R. Adam Blake
Interior design by Brian Roeth
Cover design by Brian Roeth

| METRIC CONVERSION CHART | | |
|---|---|---|
| **TO CONVERT** | **TO** | **MULTIPLY BY** |
| Inches | Centimeters | 2.54 |
| Centimeters | Inches | 0.4 |
| Feet | Centimeters | 30.5 |
| Centimeters | Feet | 0.03 |
| Yards | Meters | 0.9 |
| Meters | Yards | 1.1 |
| Sq.Inches | Sq.Centimeters | 6.45 |
| Sq.Centimeters | Sq.Inches | 0.16 |
| Sq.Feet | Sq.Meters | 0.09 |
| Sq.Meters | Sq.Feet | 10.8 |
| Sq.Yards | Sq.Meters | 0.8 |
| Sq.Meters | Sq.Yards | 1.2 |
| Pounds | Kilograms | 0.45 |
| Kilograms | Pounds | 2.2 |
| Ounces | Grams | 28.4 |
| Grams | Ounces | 0.04 |

## Acknowledgments

Woodworking is a tradition we pass on to others to keep alive the ideas and inventiveness of those who came before us. The majority of the jigs and many of the furniture designs included in this book are variations on things I have seen elsewhere in other people's shops, in books and magazines, and elsewhere. I hope the designs here are useful variations on those ideas, and worthy of the tradition they are a part of.

My father, Edward Ballou Greef, read much of the manuscript of this book and gave a lot of useful advice about how to make things clearer. He was also the first person to put woodworking tools in my hands. I have fond memories of destroying his scrap lumber as a child while he made various pieces of furniture for the family. His woodworking, like that of his father and grandfather, was practical in orientation, built as much out of need as out of a desire to create. I hope this book passes on the family tradition of woodworking as an enjoyable, utilitarian craft.

Scott Landis did a wonderful service to all woodworkers with his fine work *The Workbench Book* which I poured over for details on bench designs from the past. The tail vise design I present here is a direct descendant of the Shaker tail vise design Landis transmits to us via his book, though mine is altered to suit the needs of hobbyists.

Michael Rugg is the superb artist whose drawings you'll find in these pages. They were done with computer graphics, a lot of patience, and a real concern on the artist's part for the quality of the book.

My editors David Lewis and Adam Blake did a great deal to guide me through the quagmire of writing a first book. Behind the scenes with every book and magazine is a small army of people who do everything from layout photos on the page to locating the author's numerous misspellings. They all deserve a tip of the hat.

Thanks to my mother, Isabelle Worthington Strong, for her encouragement of my efforts.

And lastly thanks to my cat Calvin, whose serenity and indomitable here-and-now optimism should be an inspiration to us all.

## About the Author

Jeffrey Strong Greef received a B.A. in Classical Literature from the University of California, Santa Cruz, in 1981. From 1984 to 1989 he made sash and door at the Davenport Mill near Santa Cruz, making furniture in his spare time. Combining words and wood, he began to write for magazines such as *Fine Woodworking, Home Mechanix, Workbench, Popular Woodworking, Woodshop News* and others. He edited *Woodwork* magazine in 1989 and 1990, and since then has written on a strictly freelance basis. He presently lives in Santa Cruz, where he is also a disc jockey at KUSP Radio, hosting a program of international folk music.

# TABLE OF CONTENTS

# INTRODUCTION

This book is for the beginning to intermediate home hobbyist woodworker setting up a shop. One of the first questions such a person will ask is, "What machines, jigs and fixtures should I make or buy?" The answer to this lies in what kinds of projects you plan to build, the kinds of methods you prefer to employ and your budget. This book demonstrates machine tool techniques with shop-made jigs and describes various store-bought devices used to make basic furniture joints. Then these techniques are applied to constructing practical, solidly designed shop furniture, such as benches, cabinets and router tables.

The cost of woodworking machines is not cheap, and few people can afford a shop full of them. But you can make the majority of commonly used furniture joints with only a table saw, router, hand drill and various jigs, if you design your projects to conform to the capabilities of your tooling. Jointers and planers don't cut mortises and tenons, they just make straight and uniform stock, which is easier to join accurately. Most machine joinery isn't done with jointers and planers anyway, rather it is more often done with a table saw, router and jigs. A drill press also helps a great deal, and inexpensive bench-mounted models are available. You *can* do good woodworking on a budget.

The shop-made jigs in this book are mostly variations on basic ideas that have been used for years, and for the most part they represent techniques that will have broad applications for later furniture projects. You are limited in what jigs you can easily make in a woodshop however, and numerous inexpensive devices are available that give you more capability. Many of those are covered in this book. Some of those duplicate the shop-made jigs, and are here for those who prefer to buy jigs. I tried to present a wide selection of items that will be of the most use to home shop enthusiasts. The combination of shop-made and store-bought jigs gives you a broad range of possibilities to consider.

This, then, is a collection of what I think are the most useful, accessible and inexpensive machine joinery choices available to the home shop enthusiast.

The book also includes plans and instructions that apply those techniques to making the furniture you may need in your shop. The majority of this book is how-to instructions for original designs of benches, wooden vises, a grinder cabinet, storage cabinets, router tables and jigs. The projects are designed to make use of the joinery techniques that the jigs will do, and almost all of the techniques are demonstrated on one or more of the projects. Since most of the techniques covered have wide application to furniture construction, anyone who does most of what is in this book will be well prepared to tackle a large number of furniture projects, both in terms of tooling and skills.

If you are a beginner, you should be aware that machine tool woodworking is not your only alternative; hand tools can be had more cheaply than a shop full of machines, and they give almost unlimited capabilities. It is true that it takes longer to learn the skills involved, but it doesn't take so long that you should altogether ignore hand tools in favor of machines. Hand tools do some things faster than machines—like removing planer knife marks with a smoothing plane rather than a belt sander. Hand tools do some things that machines don't easily do, like shaping a cabriole leg with a spokeshave. Hand tools don't scream, rattle and make dust like routers. Overall, though, machines are far faster and easier to use. For this reason, they are the choice of many home shop hobbyists who have limited time for learning techniques and making projects. But in the long run you will be a better woodworker if you also learn about hand tools, so I suggest you learn machine and hand tool use simultaneously, gradually gaining the advantages of both.

The needs of woodworkers who use hand tools for all or most of their work are very different from the needs of those who use machine tools. Hand tool use requires devices that clamp and hold the work steady while a tool is applied to it, like a tail vise with dogs holding a board while you plane it. Machine tool use often requires a jig or fixture that guides the work while it is applied to the tool, like a tenoning jig on the table saw. But there is overlap here too—often

you want to hold a board steady while you apply a router to its edge. The joinery techniques in this book focus entirely on machine tool requirements, but the traditional bench design, with its age-old clamping methods, is applicable to both approaches.

Some of the shop furniture projects you'll find in here are fairly complicated for a beginning woodworker. You may think, "Why should I spend so much time on shop furniture? I want to get on to other projects." I've presented some easier alternatives to benches and cabinets if that is your desire, but there are two good reasons that you should consider doing the more difficult projects. First, these projects demonstrate the techniques presented with the jigs, and are an excellent learning ground for developing basic skills. You won't learn much about quality

woodworking by making simple, plywood cabinets. Secondly, better quality benches and cabinets will serve you better over time, both functionally and aesthetically. Benches take a beating, and a less sturdy bench will eventually suffer for it. And a few years from now you will regret having made simpler cabinets, because they will be beneath your advancing skills. You will probably want to make a better bench, and the time, effort and expense that went into the first will seem wasted. Do it right the first time, even if it means a few amateurish mistakes here and there.

Either way you proceed, I hope this book gives you a lot of grist for your mill and useful ideas that you will enjoy applying. Hurrah for dusty clothing!

# PART 1

# MAKING AND USING JIGS

A jig is any attachment or other device that helps you execute a certain task with a tool. It can be as simple as a block of wood with a hole bored into it used to align holes, or as complicated as some of the store-bought dovetail jigs which have intricate capabilities. Whenever you want to make a joint or any kind of cut, think to yourself, "What kind of jig might I build or buy that will make this easy, fast and accurate?" The jigs presented in this book cover many of the more common joints and cuts that a furniture maker will encounter, but when you come across an uncommon one, don't be afraid to make your own jig.

The three key factors to look at when you design a jig are *alignment*, *reference* and *adjustability*. A jig aligns a tool to a part, referring to a specific surface. That is, in order for the jig to hold a tool in the alignment that you want, it has to have some point of reference. A doweling jig aligns your drill bit to the wood at 90°. But where on the edge of the board will the bit be held at 90°? Some dowel jigs are designed to hold the bit a certain distance from a certain face on the wood. Others are designed to center the bit between two faces. Each method *refers* to a different face or faces to align the bit on the part.

When you design a jig, first decide what tool you want to use to execute the task. Which tool you use might very well depend on how easy it is to make a jig for that tool. Next look at how the tool must be aligned to the work to achieve the needed cut. Then ask the question, "What sort of platen, lever, fence, or other contrivance will hold both the part and tool simultaneously in the correct alignment to make this cut?" With that answered, decide which face or other surface of the part would be best or most convenient to refer to in order to locate your alignment correctly. Finally, construct the jig with a fence or platen which this surface can lie against and be clamped to.

Adjustability usually means being able to move the relationship between the tool and the part in very slight amounts so you can locate cuts accurately, while still retaining your proper alignment. You can use a little mechanical help for this. Whoever invented the threaded bolt gets a tip of my hat, because the mechanical advantage threads give you allows such slight movements with great accuracy and ease. On wooden jigs, you can install special metal inserts, or T-nuts, which have threads for holding bolts. By turning the bolt $1/4$ turn or so in these inserts, you can push a fence on your jig just a hair, and then retract it the same amount if you wish.

Several other modern marvels that make jig building easier are hanger bolts, toggle clamps and hardwood plywood. A hanger bolt has wood threads on one end, and bolt threads on the other , and lets you tighten down fences with wing nuts. Toggle clamps are small clamps that easily attach to jigs. And $1/4$"-thick "Baltic birch" plywood is a tough, stable material perfect for jigs. All it needs is a cheaper price tag.

Let's look at a couple of jigs in this book to see how these ideas are applied. Turn to chapter three and look at the micro adjustable tenoning jig. This jig is for cutting open mortise and tenon joints, as well as other tasks. A table saw is a good choice for such cuts, because all that is required is straight, through cuts, which a table saw does very well. But you can't make these cuts with the part lying flat on the table; it must be perpendicular to the table. You can't safely hold it with your hands, so you need a platen perpendicular to the table to hold the part aligned to the blade. The point of reference in this case is the face of the part that contacts the vertical platen.

Adjustment is a key issue with this jig, because tenon thicknesses must be carefully set to fit mortises. You must be able to move the platen back and forth in relation to the blade in slight amounts for accurate fits. It also helps to be able to adjust the platen to keep it parallel to the blade. Both of these functions are accomplished with bolts and T-nuts on this jig.

Now look at the router mortising jig in chapter ten. Making blind mortises is not a table saw job; it is better accomplished with a plunge router. This jig aligns the plunge bit to the part so that the mortise will be parallel to the outside faces of the part. The jig refers to one face of the part, much as the table saw tenoning jig does. This jig allows you to adjust the relation between the bit and the work by positioning the router base with fences. These fences are themselves moved with the use of bolts and threaded inserts.

The function of a jig, then, is to line everything up for you to make the job easy. Once it is lined up and ready, you should be able to make consistent cuts on parts in rapid succession. In cabinet shops, jigs are frequently used in production arrangements for efficiently making numerous identical furniture parts. This kind of accurate duplication is the main advantage of machine technology. In effect, the only real difference between a woodworking machine and your shop-made jig is the degree of specialization of each. Think of yourself as a specialized toolmaker.

# 1 PLANNING AND LAYING OUT YOUR SHOP

## Buy Only What You Need

When you begin accumulating tools and jigs, buy and make only what you need for your immediate projects. This may mean buying items that seem rather unromantic, like sharpening stones or a variable-speed electric drill. However, you must have essentials like these, and accumulating them will take a fair amount of money. But by far the most important decision you'll make at the beginning is what machines to buy.

## What Machines Should I Buy?

There are many types, sizes and brands of woodworking machines available, and prices vary widely. To decide what you will get, focus on three factors: what capabilities you need, the quality of machine you want and your budget.

**Table Saw.** A table saw quickly and accurately cuts a smooth, straight line on the edge of stock. It's the best single tool for both ripping parts to width and cross cutting them. It will also do much joinery with the use of various jigs. A table saw should be the first machine you buy for doing machine tool woodworking.

Capacity of table saws is measured by blade diameter, motor power and distance the fence will move away from the blade. Common blade sizes are 8¼, 10 and 12 inch. Get a 10 inch—it will handle your needs. A 1½ horsepower motor will suffice for most work, but a 2 or 3 horsepower will serve far better for thick stock. Some machines have fence extensions that locate the fence 4 feet from the blade. This is handy if you will be cutting a lot of plywood.

Get a good quality carbide-toothed combination blade for your saw. They are expensive, but rarely need sharpening and will last a lifetime with moderate use.

Your second machine purchase may be a toss-up between a band saw and a drill press. For the projects in this book, a drill press will be more useful, because this book presents practical projects that avoid curved frills and use joinery that a drill press excels at.

**Drill Press.** Because it bores well-aligned holes, a drill press is a big help for most (not all) doweling

and mortising. Chisel mortising attachments allow you to make square holes. Capacities for drill presses are measured by the distance from the chuck center to the support post, as well as the total throw, or how deep a hole it will cut.

**Band Saw.** A band saw will cut both curved and straight lines, but it is not as good at straight lines as a table saw, because the thin blade can wander, distorting the cut. A band saw can cut much thicker stock than a table saw, and so it is good for resawing thick pieces into thin ones, and breaking down heavy chunks.

The capacity of band saws is measured by the horizontal distance from the blade to the arm. Common sizes are 14 and 16 inches. The second capacity of a band saw is the maximum height that it will cut. This is only critical if you plan to resaw wide boards.

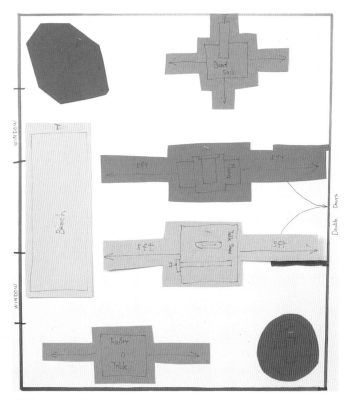

*Make a scale floor plan of your shop area, as well as cutout figures representing your tools, benches, etc. Move the figures about on the floor plan to determine the best arrangement to avoid conflicts.*

A major factor to consider when buying a band saw is how much curved work you plan on doing. You can do a limited amount of curved work with scroll saws and saber saws, but a band saw does most of what they will do plus much more.

**Planer.** A planer reduces and evens the thickness of a piece of lumber. A planer does not make a board flat, it evens out the thickness following the contour of the face placed against its platen. Warped stock in, warped stock out.

Planer capacity is measured in the width of cut, as well as how deep it will cut. Ten and 12 inch models are available now, and these usually have minimally powered motors that don't cut very deep on each pass, but will do the job. It is possible to do without a planer by finding a shop that will plane for you, or by designing your projects around available stock thicknesses.

**Jointer.** One of the simplest of machines, a jointer makes a straight line or plane where there was an irregular one before. It will do this on a board's edge or face. However, it will not accurately even out the thickness of lumber. For that you need a planer.

The primary capacity of a jointer is the width of cut, or how long the knives are. Common sizes are 4, 6, and 8 inches. This capacity determines how wide a piece of lumber you can face joint, or make flat on the face. Remember that when you face joint, you must afterwards use a planer to even out the thickness.

Another feature on some jointers is an adjustable outfeed table, which lets you turn a wheel to easily adjust the relationship between the height of the knives and the height of the outfeed table. This adjustment is critical for getting a straight cut.

**Radial Arm Saw.** This tool makes accurate crosscuts more conveniently than a table saw. It will make angled crosscuts and dadoes, and can be used for ripping stock along its width—though this is far easier and more accurate on a table saw. Like a table saw, the blade size is the most important capacity consideration on a radial arm. Get a 10 inch. Radial arm saws take up a lot of room, so get one only if you have the space.

**Sanders.** Stationary belt and disc sanders are handy for shaping curved parts and smoothing rough edges. There are a variety of types.

**Scroll Saws.** A reciprocating thin blade makes fine cuts, following curves around very tight corners. It can also cut holes in the middle of stock—unlike a band saw. Not very useful for joinery, scroll saws excel at cutting attractive frills. Capacity of scroll saws is measured by throat distance like a band saw, and length of throw of the blade.

*You need good measuring tools to do accurate work with machines. Along with a tape measure, get a calipers for telling you exact thicknesses, as well as a 6" steel rule for carefully measuring small distances.*

**Lathe.** Lathes are used for turning spindle legs, bowls, cups, and other such round objects. The capacity is measured by the distance from the lathe center to the lathe bed. This capacity determines the maximum diameter, or width, of a piece that can be fitted onto the machine. The bed length determines the maximum length of the piece.

**Shaper.** Primarily for shaping curved contours on edges or faces of stock, a shaper is also useful for straight cuts like rabbeting. Shaper capacity is measured by the diameter of the shaft and the power of the motor. A router table is an excellent substitute for a shaper for most such tasks, and can be easily built rather than bought.

For the home shop woodworker, a combination machine can be a good choice. It requires less space than several separate machines and costs less than two or more machines.

You should also consider used machines, which regularly appear in your newspaper's want ads. Be sure to use a machine before you buy it, and inspect it carefully for broken castings and other evidence of damage. Old, heavy-duty machines can be tempting, but they can cost more to refurbish than a smaller new machine.

**Machine Quality.** Many less expensive import machines are available now, and the prices are very

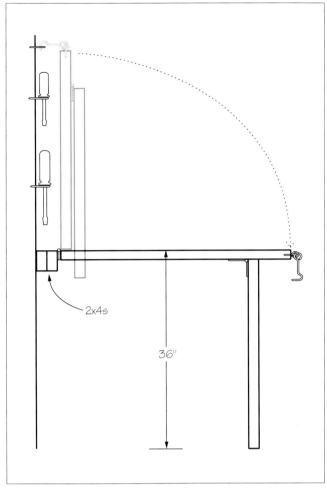

*In a very small shop, such as a one-car garage, make a bench that folds up and out of the way when not in use. For a bench top use a 36" solid core door. Attach it with hinges away from the wall far enough that you can fit tools between it and the wall when the bench is up.*

**Dust Collectors.** Installing a dust collector is a good idea for health reasons and for reducing time spent sweeping. But dust collectors and ducting are expensive. A system attached to four or five machines can cost well over one thousand dollars.

Setting up a large system of ducting involves making lengthy mathematical calculations; you must determine how powerful a motor and fan you need to pull air through all that ducting. Ducting introduces resistance to the flow of air, so the more ducting you have, the bigger motor and fan you need. If you choose to set up a large system, see the list of suppliers at the end of the book which contains names of various collector manufacturers who publish literature on how to make the necessary calculations.

But there is a simpler approach. If you don't have all that ducting, there is less resistance in your system, so you need a lower capacity collector. Consider buying a less expensive, low-capacity model mounted on a dolly (or mount it yourself), and wheel it around the shop to whatever machine you are using. Attach the machine with a short length of flexible hose.

Another alternative is to connect only the worst dust offenders, like your table saw and power sander, to the collector. If you have only two machines connected to the collector, position them close to the collector so you have a minimum of ducting to install, reducing the cost and the needed capacity of the collector.

## Arranging Tools in Your Shop

How you arrange your tools and furniture in the shop is important to give you as much capability as possible and to avoid frustrating and dangerous conflicts. Make a scale floor plan of your available shop space, then make scaled paper cutout figures of each machine. Include in the cutouts not only the top-view shape of the machine, but also arrows (in front of and behind the machine) which show the paths that wood will follow as it is passed across the machine. See the photo on page 4. Arrange your cutouts on your scale drawing. Shuffle them around until you come up with an arrangement that allows plenty of room around the areas where stock will go into and come out of machines.

Place the table saw or planer close to a door so long boards can go outside as they come out of the machine. Or, cut a hole in the wall, and cover it with a small door. Open the door only when you need to let stock go the extra distance.

If you have little space, consider putting your machines on rollers. Make double-layer ³⁄₄" plywood platens for the machines to rest on, and invest in

attractive. The key here is simple—you get what you pay for. For instance, cast iron moves as it ages, and companies making less expensive machines usually don't let the castings age long enough to guarantee minimal movement. This doesn't mean less expensive machines have warped tables—it means they could, and warped tables on a jointer, for instance, can render the machine useless. In practical experience this rarely happens, but you should ask for a guarantee that tables will stay flat on any machine with large, flat castings, such as table saws and jointers.

You will probably find the quality of handles and other attachments lesser on inexpensive machines. Service after the sale may be less than you would prefer. You may need to fiddle around with the machine to get it to work right. But the less expensive machines work, and if it's the difference between having a machine and not having a machine, the choice is obvious.

good quality rollers from the hardware store. Some rollers have locking tabs that fix the wheels in place.

**Safety.** Safety is an attitude that you bring into your shop. All the special procedures and guards in the world aren't worth a darn if you don't *constantly* pay attention to what you are doing. There is always a safe way to do it, but often it takes longer to set up the extra jig or fence that makes it safe. Whether you take that time is up to you.

Roll up your sleeves so your cuff doesn't get caught in a blade. Tie back long hair or beards. Wear safety glasses or goggles, and when using a lathe wear a face mask. Remove rings and watches from your hands so they don't get caught in machines. Long-term exposure to loud noises will impair your hearing, so use ear protection. Dust is not good for your respiratory system, so wear that mask and/or install a dust collection system.

Do not use drugs or alcohol when using machines. Some medicine labels warn against using machinery while taking the drug. Read the labels.

The following is a list of potential hazards on specific machines. This list is not comprehensive, and you can encounter other hazards. Be aware.

**Table Saw.** Keep your eye on the blade and on your fingers so you don't push your fingers into the blade. Use push sticks for stock less than 3" wide. Always hold stock firmly as it is cut, because if the blade grabs the piece it can throw it backwards hard. Don't stand directly behind the work while it is being cut. Don't rip pieces shorter than 18" at the table saw.

**Drill Press.** If the bit grabs your work, it will spin it around like a propeller. Clamp work down, or butt it against a clamped fence. Keep clothes and hair away from the bit.

**Band saw.** As with the table saw, keep your eye on the blade and on your fingers. Don't retract the cut while the blade is spinning, or else you may pull the spinning blade off the wheels in which case it can break and whip about.

**Planer.** Don't stick your hand in the planer or lift the guard while it's on. A planer can throw stock backwards if it gets loose beneath the rollers, so don't stand directly behind the machine.

**Jointer.** Don't pass your hands over the cutter head, and don't joint stock less than 18" in length.

**Radial Arm Saw.** Never place your arm or hand along the path of cut. Your right hand holds the handle, your left holds the stock to the left of the blade. Don't cut short parts.

## Buying Lumber for the Projects in This Book

If you can afford to, buy a large quantity of lumber at once to cover several projects. In the long run you'll save money, because you will be able to use the lumber more efficiently, as well as get a price break on quantity. Here is some advice on how to proceed.

I'm assuming that you do not have a jointer and a planer, so the projects are structured around using surfaced 1× (one-by) lumber, whose actual thickness is ¾" or ¹³⁄₁₆". But if you do have a jointer and a planer, you should buy unsurfaced lumber, often called "full sawn," which is close to 1" thickness. This way you can face joint your stock to flatten it, and then plane it to ¾" thickness for the projects.

Without a jointer and a planer, however, you cannot flatten stock. Therefore it becomes very important that you find flat pieces for situations where flatness is critical. One reason for buying a large amount of lumber at once is that you can pick through it and find the flat pieces and not-so-flat ones, and use each where appropriate. If a lumber yard will let you pick through its stock, do so.

A board that isn't flat isn't useless. Often it can be cut into short parts where the distortion does not show because the part is small. And, for projects that require stack lamination, you can glue together warped boards and get a flat result. The traditional bench design I present in this book uses this lamination technique for almost all of its parts, as does a router table top. You can also use knots in the bench component laminations and they'll still be strong—an excellent way to make efficient use of cheaper, knotted stock.

Consider purchasing number 1 common grade lumber. This is a less expensive, lower grade of lumber, which has a certain number of knots, splits and other defects. Because the projects in this book mostly call for small parts, you can carefully plan how to cut each board between defects to make maximum use of each piece.

Finally, what kind of lumber should you use? Just about any will do, but very soft woods like pine won't hold up well over time. I used alder for most of what's in this book. It's cheap, and looks a bit like cherry minus the red. What you use matters mostly from the standpoints of cost and aesthetics—you don't want to break the bank, but remember that you will be looking at this furniture for years to come, so you may want to pick your favorite wood.

# 2 CROSSCUTTING WITH YOUR MITER GAUGE

The miter gauge you get with your table saw is capable of aligning parts for cuts at angles from 0° to 45°. You may find, however, that you'll use it at least as much set at 90° (or call it 0°, if you like) as for other angles. In this respect the name "miter gauge" is a bit of a misnomer, since for 90° cuts it is being used only to function as a support mechanism for right angles, not for its ability to align miters. The tool functions very well as a support and is a necessary safety device for crosscuts made without a larger cutoff box (see chapter eight).

You can use the miter gauge to cut parts to length

**Photo 1—Don't butt stock against the rip fence when you cut off short parts with a miter gauge, because the blade might catch the loose parts and throw them. Use a reference block before the blade to orient the cut and give distance between the fence and part.**

for your projects, but it is not large enough to support long or large parts very well. For those jobs it is best to make a cutoff box, which provides better support. But when you need to cut off short parts, the miter gauge used with your rip fence and a reference block is a good way to go.

It's tempting when cutting short parts to set the rip

fence at the desired distance from the blade, then butt the end of the part against the rip fence and push through using the miter gauge for support. But this is potentially dangerous, because once the short part is cut free, it is left between the blade and fence with no clearance and can get jammed and thrown by the blade. For this reason, clamp a reference block to the rip fence well ahead of the blade, as shown in the photo on page 8. Set the distance from the reference block to the blade at your desired part length. Butt the end of your stock against the reference block, hold the stock firmly onto the gauge, and push it through.

If you are concerned about tearout on your short parts, attach a backup fence to the miter gauge with screws. This fence must extend from the gauge to beyond the blade, and must be tall enough so the blade doesn't cut it off. Such a backup fence will have the added convenience of pushing the cutoff part ahead of the blade. Without a backup fence, your short parts will be left between the blade and fence, but with some distance between so it is less likely to get caught. It still can get caught, though, so use a backup fence or push stick to clear it before you make the next cut.

You can use a similar setup to cut tenons (see the photo at right). Mount a dado cutter into the saw, and set the rip fence from the outside of the blade at the dimension you want for your tenon length. Mount a backup fence on the miter gauge. Place your parts facedown on the table saw, and raise the cutter to a height equal to the tenon shoulder dimension. Turn on the saw and make the first cut with the end of the part against the rip fence. You don't need a reference fence as with cutting off, since no parts will be cut free of the part other than dust and chips.

After the first cut, retract the part, and slide it away from the rip fence about ¾". Make another cut, and repeat the procedure until you have removed all waste from that side of the tenon. Then, flip the part and do the other side.

Notice that the exact thickness of the resulting

*Photo 2—Make tenons with the miter gauge and a dado set using this setup. The backup piece screwed to the miter gauge reduces tearout on the tenon shoulder.*

tenon depends on the height of the dado cutter in the saw. To fit your tenons to your mortises, make the first one too thick to begin with, then raise the cutter a hair, pass it through again, and test the fit. Repeat this procedure until you get a good fit. But don't assume that the setting you have will work for all your tenons. The thickness of the parts also contributes to the final thickness of the tenon, and varying part thicknesses means varying tenon thicknesses. Note that the dado cutter leaves a rough surface on the tenon face. Overall, this is the least precise machine method for making tenons—but it's the fastest and will do in a pinch.

# 3 MICRO ADJUSTABLE TENONING JIG

This heavy-duty jig lets you make accurate mortise and tenon joints, as well as other joints, at the table saw.

**T**his jig holds parts vertically at the table saw so you can make various cuts on the ends of the parts. One of the most common of these kinds of cuts is making tenons, but you can also use this jig to cut mortises, slots for splines and the like. Note that the only kind of mortise you can cut with this kind of arrangement is an open mortise, but the tenons made hereon can be used with open or closed ("blind") mortises. A tenon is a tenon.

To make accurate cuts this jig must hold the part parallel to the blade and vertical to the saw table. There are three factors here. First, both the blade and the carrier face of the jig must be at 90° to the saw table. When you make the carrier, you establish this permanent 90° setting. Secondly, you must attach a fence to the carrier face, the edge of which is at 90° to the saw table. Lastly, the front and rear of the carrier face must be the same distance from the blade, so that the carrier is parallel to the blade. You adjust this setting on the jig using the four bolts on the front and rear edges of the jig base. These align the wooden ways that hold the carrier assembly within the base, which in turn aligns the carrier to the blade.

To adjust the distance of the carrier from the blade, loosen the securing bolts that hold the carrier to the base, and turn the single long bolt on the back side of the jig. The spring in the center of the jig pushes the carrier against this adjustment bolt, so that as you retract the bolt, the carrier retracts with it.

Begin the jig by cutting out the plywood parts for both the carrier and the base. Follow the dimensions on the drawing to mark out the two base pieces, and cut out the curves with a band, scroll or saber saw. For the carrier, cut out three rectangles as shown on the cutout list: one for the carrier bottom and two for the vertical carrier face.

You must cut out five holes in the middle of the carrier bottom. Four of these are for the securing bolts to pass through, the fifth is for the spring block (as shown in photo 1 on page 13). Mark the locations of these holes using the dimensions shown in the drawing. Drill holes within your marks, then use a scroll or saber saw to clear out the waste. Mark a ½" hole for the spring dowel along the bottom edge of one of the two vertical carrier face pieces. Center the hole from side to side, and bore it ½" above the bottom edge.

Make the triangular supports for the vertical carrier face out of solid stock, which takes screws better in the edges than plywood. Cut the supports out on the table saw using the miter gauge, or miter cutoff box, set at 45°. For safety, start with a piece at least 30" long so you have plenty to grip while you make the cut. Orient the grain of the parts parallel to the diagonal side of the triangles. The combination of two 45° cuts for each triangle should yield a 90° angle between the horizontal and vertical edges of the parts. Be sure this is 90°. If it is not, adjust the edges with a stationary sander, but don't adjust them on the table saw because now they are too short. Screw the triangles to the carrier face. Your parts should appear as in photo 1 on page 13.

Make the two U-shaped frames that fit on the carrier and on the base out of short hardwood scrap pieces. Join them at the corners with a groove and

*You install T-nuts and bolts on the tenoning jig to give it the minute adjustments required for accurate fits between mortises and tenons.*

tenon joint. Cut ¼" wide grooves ½" deep on the ends of the parts shown in the drawing using a dado set in the table saw. Cut the groove into the ends only far enough to accommodate the tenon, not along the entire edge. Note that the grooves on the base piece need to be a bit longer so the tenon on the loose way will have room, as in photo 4 (page 14). Cut corresponding tenons on the meeting parts using the tenoning setup covered in chapter seven. Make the moveable ways at this time too, since their tenons fit in the same groove.

Before you glue up the U frames, bore holes for the bolt slots in the carrier U frame pieces as you did in the carrier plywood bottom. Bore a ½" hole on the inside edge of the carrier U frame bottom for the spring dowel. Make it ⅜" deep, centered along the length of the part, and its center at ½" up from the bottom.

Next bore holes for the adjustment bolts and locator dowels on the base U frame pieces. Install T-nuts for the adjustment bolts, and recess the heads of these nuts within the face of the part by making a shallow cut with a wide drill bit where the head will reside. The locator dowels hold the moveable ways in place. Glue up the two U frames. Make sure that the joints are at 90°. Let the glue dry.

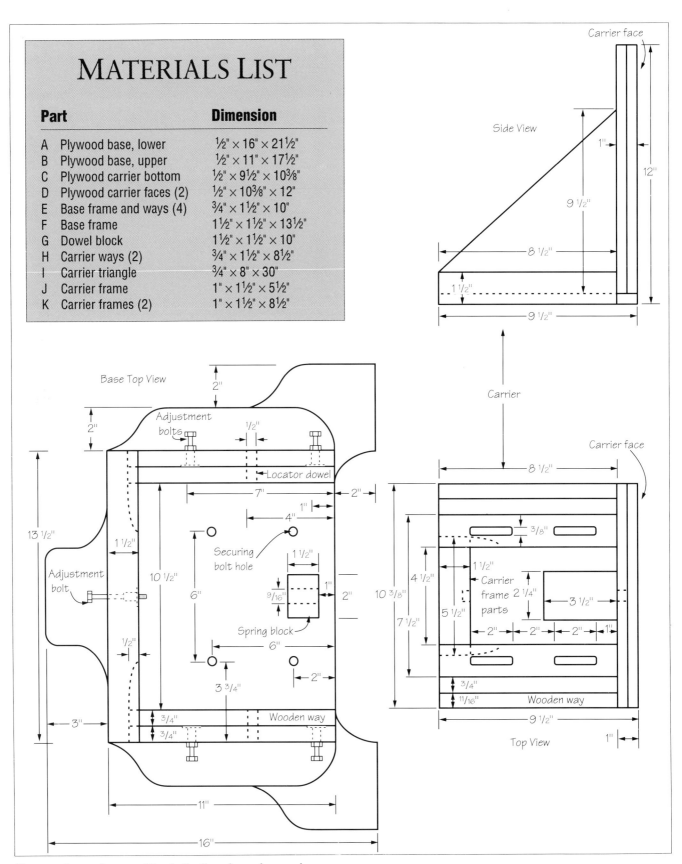

## MATERIALS LIST

| Part | | Dimension |
|------|-----|-----------|
| A | Plywood base, lower | ½" × 16" × 21½" |
| B | Plywood base, upper | ½" × 11" × 17½" |
| C | Plywood carrier bottom | ½" × 9½" × 10⅜" |
| D | Plywood carrier faces (2) | ½" × 10⅜" × 12" |
| E | Base frame and ways (4) | ¾" × 1½" × 10" |
| F | Base frame | 1½" × 1½" × 13½" |
| G | Dowel block | 1½" × 1½" × 10" |
| H | Carrier ways (2) | ¾" × 1½" × 8½" |
| I | Carrier triangle | ¾" × 8" × 30" |
| J | Carrier frame | 1" × 1½" × 5½" |
| K | Carrier frames (2) | 1" × 1½" × 8½" |

*There are two main assemblies to the jig: a larger base and a carrier that fits within the base.*

Photo 1—Cut holes in the carrier base bottom for the securing bolts and dowel block to pass through. Attach triangular supports to one of the two vertical carrier faces, which has a hole bored for the spring dowel.

Photo 2—Make the carrier U-frame and base U-frame at the same time, because the joinery for both is the same. Attach the carrier U-frame to the carrier bottom with screws from below.

Photo 3 Screw the carrier triangles and vertical face assembly to the carrier U-frame, and then screw the carrier ways onto the outer edge of the triangles.

Place the carrier U frame on the carrier bottom plywood piece, flush to the rear and centered side to side as in photo 2. Screw the triangular base pieces to the first vertical carrier face, and make the two fixed ways that attach to the side of the carrier. Screw all of these together as in the photo (above right).

Bore holes in the plywood top base piece for T-nuts that will hold the carrier securing bolts to the base. Use the dimensions shown in the drawing to position these holes. Place the T-nuts on the bottom of the plywood, and recess them into the bottom as you did with the other T-nuts so they won't hit the lower plywood base when it is installed.

Make the spring block by first cutting out a piece at 1½"×1½"×10". Bore a ⁹⁄₁₆" hole in the middle of this piece, with the hole center at 1" above the bottom face. Now cut the part to length at 2" with a cutoff box, cutting so that the hole ends up along the center of the short length of the piece. Screw this piece to the top base piece as shown in photo 4 (page 14).

Place the base U frame on the top base plywood, and adjust it so that its sides are equidistant and parallel to the T-nut holes in the plywood. (It's more important that the U frame be oriented to these holes rather than to the sides of the plywood.) Clamp it in place and screw it to the plywood from below. Insert the short locator dowels in their holes in the U frame, and place the ways on those dowels with their tenons in the slots along the U frame bottom. Trim the tenon

faces with a chisel so they will slide within the grooves. Your base assembly should appear as in photo 4 (page 14).

Place the carrier assembly within the base U frame and ways as in photo 5 (page 14). The carrier should slide freely back and forth within the ways. There should be no interference between the spring block and the carrier bottom. The securing bolt slots in the carrier should be located directly over the T-nut holes in the base. Install the securing bolts. Cut them short if they protrude below the bottom of the T-nuts when they are tightened. When these bolts are loose, the carrier should slide freely back and forth. If there is resistance, try adjusting the ways to push the carrier to a position where there is no resistance. If there is still resistance, find the rubbing surfaces and reduce the surrounding wood with a chisel.

Push the spring dowel through its hole in the carrier face and through the spring block. It should seat in the hole in the carrier U frame bottom without contacting the spring block. If the spring dowel does rub against the spring block, try adjusting the way locations to center the dowel in the block. Place the springs onto the dowel as you push it into place, as in photo 6 (page 14).

Screw the second vertical carrier face over the first, thus securing the dowel in place. Screw the bottom base piece to the assembly. Take your favorite handsaw and trace the pattern of its handle onto a thick

*Photo 4—Screw the base U-frame to the upper plywood base with screws from below. Note that the base ways fit loosely in the frame and are kept in place with locator dowels and unglued tenons.*

*Photo 5—Place the carrier within the base, adjust the ways, and check that the carrier slides freely within the base ways.*

*Photo 6—Attach a handle to the rear triangular support. Install the retracting springs as you insert the dowel from in front of the carrier face.*

piece of scrap. Cut out the profile with a band saw or scroll saw. If you do not have a scroll saw, cut out the center hole by boring numerous holes in the area and then chiseling the waste. Screw the handle to the aft triangular support, and be sure that it does not rub against the base ways below it.

Measure the distance from your table saw blade to the miter gauge slot on the saw table top. Make a wood guide that fits snugly within the slot, but still slides easily within. Screw this slide to the bottom of the jig, and place it from the cutting edge of the jig at the same distance as the slot is from the blade. Position the guide so that it is parallel to the carrier face.

Place the jig on the table saw within the guide slot. Raise your blade to about 2", and place the jig alongside the blade. Now carefully measure the distance of the carrier from the blade both at the front of the blade and at the rear. If these two dimensions are not equal, adjust the position of the carrier in the base using the adjustment bolts on either side of the jig. Adjust the bolts so that the carrier can slide easily toward and away from the blade, but without any slop between ways so that it stays parallel to the blade no matter where it is.

## Making Mortises and Tenons

First, rip your stock to width and cut it to length. Don't forget to include the length of tenons on parts that have them. Next, determine the approximate thickness of the tenons you intend to make. Traditionally, tenons are made at one-third the thickness of the stock, but I like to make them just a bit thicker for more strength. I usually make tenons between $1/2$ and $1/3$ of the part thickness.

On $3/4$"-thick parts, this translates into $5/16$"-thick tenons. Before setting up with the tenoning jig, cut the shoulders of the tenons using the miter gauge on the table saw as shown in chapter seven. But don't cut through the parts; cut only $3/16$" into them to establish the tenon shoulders.

Now set up the tenoning jig. Install a vertical fence and toggle clamp on the face of the jig to hold parts firmly in place. Load a part into the jig, and adjust the distance of the carrier to the blade such that the cut will make the tenon oversize. Cut both sides of the tenon, then measure the actual thickness. Make slight adjustments and more cuts with the jig until the tenon comes to the thickness you want.

Cut mortises the same way, except skip the first step on the miter gauge cutting shoulders. Carefully adjust the width of the mortise to fit the tenons. The fit should be snug, but not so tight that you risk splitting the mortise. You could just as easily fit the tenons to the mortises. If your project calls for closed mortises, you may find that it is best to fit the tenons to the mortises since the mortise width may be fixed by the size of the cutter that makes it.

# 4 TAPERING JIG

A tapering jig rides against your table saw fence, and holds stock at an angle to the fence so that the blade will cut the stock at that angle. A common use for such a jig is cutting tapers on the edge of stock for table legs. The jig is adjustable to cut a variety of angles, and can be made to cut greater angles with a larger adjustment plate.

The basic parts of the jig are two boards attached with a hinge: a plywood base to which one is attached, and an adjustment plate with a curved slot for a hanger bolt and wing nut. The purpose of the plywood base is to make room between the table saw fence and the first board for the adjustment plate, which hangs over that board. Therefore, the plywood base needs to be wide enough to accommodate your adjustment plate.

Make the curved slot in the adjustment plate using the router radiusing jig described in chapter fourteen. Use good quality birch plywood for this piece. Remember that the center of radius must be located at the hinge pin. If it isn't, the slot will not remain over the same spot as it slides over the fixed board, and the slot edges will collide with the hanger bolt. Carefully align the slot so that all points along its arc are the same distance from the hinge pin.

You can make a tapering jig to any dimensions you desire. For most uses, a jig with the following dimensions will do. Make the two hinged boards from pieces that are ¾"×2"×30". For an adjustment plate that is a total of 8" wide, use a plywood base that is 7" wide.

When you cut tapers in table legs, notice that when you flip the part to cut the taper in the opposite side, that you now have a tapered side toward the jig. This is a problem, because to properly align the second cut, the center of the leg must be held parallel to the

*Make tapered table legs using the tapering jig.*

jig fence. The solution is to take the tapered ripping from the first cut, and wedge it in place between the jig and part.

When using this jig, be very careful about where you position your hands during the cut. Because the blade hits the part at an angle, it's hard to tell where the blade will come out of the part. You don't want your fingers there when it does. Measure before you cut so you know where the blade will leave the cut, and keep your fingers clear of the blade.

# 5 STRAIGHTEDGE JIG

*Use this jig on your table saw to straighten the edges of your stock.*

he first step in any project is to rough out your parts. To do that your stock must have a straight line on one edge. You then place this edge against the table saw fence and rip the other edge straight. But how do you get that first edge straight? Some stock comes with one edge "straightened," but often that edge is less than satisfactory. A jointer is the ideal tool to give you that first edge. If you don't have a jointer, you can build a straightedge jig for the table saw, which will let you put a straight edge on almost any board.

The jig is simply a board with a straight edge that rides against the table saw fence, along with several toggle clamps that attach your stock to the jig. With the two clamped together, the straight edge on the jig becomes the reference point that establishes the straight cut on your stock.

But how do you get a straight line onto the jig itself to begin with, if all your stock is rough? You've got several options. First, if you are pretty good with a hand plane, use it to make your straight edge. Hand planes with longer soles are best for straightening edges, but you could get a straight edge with a small smoothing plane. Secondly, make the jig from a piece of ¾" plywood that already has a straight edge on it. Lastly, go to a cabinet shop and ask them to straighten a board for you on their jointer. They will more likely do this than straighten all your stock, and once you have the jig, you won't have to go back to them again.

Make the jig base from a piece of plywood or solid stock that is about 6" wide. Any wider and it will only be useful for wide stock; if it's too narrow it won't provide much support for wide pieces. Make the piece 8' long so the jig will accommodate long stock. Screw support spacers to the base for the toggle clamps to sit on. Position these adjacent to the straight edge, but be sure that the toggle clamps will be located away from the edge so they won't hit the table saw fence.

Note that to use the jig with thick stock, the toggle clamp spacers must be at least as thick as the stock. If you plan to straighten 2× stock, make the spacers 2" thick. The adjustment bolts on the toggles will allow you to put ¾" stock into the jig with these spacers in place.

Before you use the jig, look closely at the piece of stock that you want to straighten. Where you make this first straight cut may determine what specific sizes of parts you can get out of the stock. This applies mostly to boards that have a taper on them, and you have to decide which side of the taper will be ripped off and which side becomes a straight line. Look at the boards with an eye to the ripping cut you will make after the first straight line cut. Make the straight line cut so that the rip cuts will remove defects and leave a maximum width of clear, useful stock.

You don't need to clean up the entire edge with this first cut, and it's a good idea not to. Just clean up

enough of the edge so that you have a straight line to run against the saw fence for the second cut. Later you can clean up the entire edge. At this early stage you may not know exactly which parts you will take out of this stock, so you should leave it as wide as you can to ensure maximum possibilities. Remember that you can occasionally use lumber with partly rough edges in hidden areas on your furniture, saving your better stock for high-profile areas.

Don't be afraid to cross cut your stock before you put a straight edge on it. This can save you a lot of stock on a board that is bowed to begin with. To straighten a bow on an 8' board, you must remove much stock on the ends or the middle, depending on which side you straighten. If you cut it in half first, the amount you remove from each edge in straightening is lessened significantly. When you cross cut a board first, look carefully at the part lengths that you need for your project, and make the crosscut in a location that gives you the lengths you need, or multiples thereof.

When you clamp your stock into the jig, remember that the cut will be parallel to the straight edge of the jig. Position the stock so that the line you want to cut is parallel to that edge. Adjust the toggle clamps so they hold the stock securely to the base. This jig is long and heavy once it is loaded with your stock, so you will need an extension table on your saw to hold it when the cut is over. While making the cut, keep a close eye on where the jig contacts the table saw fence, and be sure that it keeps contact throughout the cut.

*The jig consists of a long board which has a straight edge and toggle clamps mounted to it. The straight edge of the jig runs against the fence, referencing the cut.*

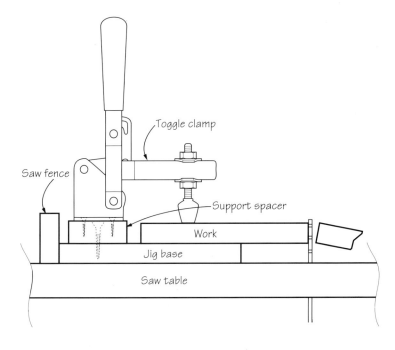

Toggle clamp

Saw fence

Support spacer

Work

Jig base

Saw table

# 6 MAKING FINGER JOINTS

This is a relatively simple jig setup that makes an attractive and very strong glue joint. It takes very little time to set up on the table saw with your miter gauge, but it can take some time to adjust correctly so that the fingers fit together just so. Once the jig is set up and adjusted however, you can easily use it to make as many tightly fitting joints as you are willing to stand there and cut.

The jig consists of three parts. The first two pieces are a base board and a slider board, which you can make from ¾"-thick stock that is at least 5" wide. The length of these pieces should be equal and

*Locate a finger tab in a slot adjacent to the path of the blade. Slide the board that holds this tab right or left until the distance of the tab from the blade equals the width of the cut made by the blade.*

depends on how wide your finger jointed boards will be. The pieces need to be long enough so that the clamps holding them together are away from the parts being cut. If you make finger joints on very wide boards, you will need longer base and slider boards.

The third piece is a finger tab that you fit in a slot within the slider board. The thickness of this tab must be the same as the thickness of the cutter that makes

*Use the finger tab to reference each cut. Place the last cut over the finger and hold it firmly in place while you push the part through the blade. Watch each cut as it is made, and keep your fingers away from the blade!*

the fingers and slots. You can use whatever thickness you choose—from the width of a saw blade to a ¾" dado, depending on what kind of fingers you want. Determine what cutter you will use. Make a sample groove with the cutter, and make finger tab stock that fits snugly into the groove.

Screw the base board to your miter gauge. Set the gauge at 90° to the blade. The base board must extend beyond the blade on the opposite side of the miter gauge by the width of your widest stock plus 2" for a clamp. Clamp the slider board onto the base board, with the ends of the slider at about ½" to the right of the base board ends. Install your cutter into the saw, and raise it just over the thickness of the parts that will get the finger joints. Cut a slot through the base and slider boards by pushing them through the saw and retracting.

Turn off the saw. Loosen the clamps, and move the slider to the left so that the groove is spaced away from the cutter at a distance equal to the width of the groove. Tighten the clamps. Place a short length of finger tab into the groove in the slider board. It cannot be higher than the thickness of the stock that gets the joints, and must fit snugly into the groove so that it won't rattle free.

Get several test pieces of stock that are the same thickness as your project parts. Don't start with your actual parts, because the first few cuts will be wrong and useless, except to show you how to adjust the

setup. Place a test piece on end in the jig, with its edge against the finger tab. Turn on the saw and, holding the part firmly to the slider board, push the part through the cutter. Wear safety glasses, and keep your eye on the cutter to be sure your fingers are not in the path of the blade. Your fingers should be high up on the part, and not down close to the table where the blade is.

After this first cut, retract the jig to a foot or more before the blade. Lift the part up and place the freshly cut slot over the finger tab. Again push it through, then retract, place the fresh slot over the tab until you have cut slots along the whole length of the part end.

The object of the setup is to make fingers that are the same thickness as the grooves between them. Note that the distance the finger tab is from the cutter determines the thickness of the fingers, but the width of the slots remains constant. Therefore, the exact location of the finger tab is crucial to the fit of the joint. Make the same cuts on a separate board, and try to fit the two together. Unless you are very lucky, they won't fit because the fingers are either too fat or too thin.

Move the slider board one way or the other to adjust the thickness of the fingers appropriately. To do so, loosen the clamps that hold the slider to the base, but not enough so that it moves freely, only enough so that the clamps exert a minimum of pressure on the two boards. Make a pencil line on top of the two boards. Take a light hammer and gently tap the slider in the direction you want it to go. Tap it very gently at first, keeping your eye on the pencil line. Tap until you see the line move just a hair, then firm up the clamps and make more cuts on test pieces. The slightest movement of the slider has a dramatic effect on the fit of the pieces, so beware of moving it much.

With a bit of testing you'll get a good fit. When you are satisfied, begin with your parts. Note that whenever you start a piece, the edge has a finger. The part that fits to this first piece must have a slot in this location. For the first cut on the second board of each joint, place an extra piece of finger tab stock between the finger tab and the part. This will cause the first cut to align with the edge of the part.

Be careful that you hold the parts in the jig the same way through all the cuts. If you begin pushing them to one side, the slight difference in position will magnify through the progression of cuts to produce ill-fitting joints. Conversely, if you notice that your joints seem to be just a hair too tight, you can intentionally push the parts to one side just a bit as you hold them in place, slightly loosening the fit.

# 7 SIMPLE TABLE SAW TENONING JIG

This tenoning jig is a condensed version of its larger brother shown in chapter three. Like the larger jig, this design uses a bolt with a T-nut to adjust the distance of the carrier from the blade for tuning in the thicknesses of tenons and widths of mortises. It is lighter than the larger one, and is a good choice if you have only a few joints to make, or if you just want to spend less time making such a jig.

Though it is much simpler to make, it has the disadvantage of being unadjustable for all of its alignments, except distance to the blade. The larger jig allows you to adjust with minute accuracy the position of the carrier on the base, so you can easily guarantee that the carrier is parallel to the blade. With this smaller model you must make the carrier parallel to the blade by carefully locating the positions of all the parts on the jig before you screw them down. If you miss this alignment, your tenons and mortises won't be square along all their dimensions, and they won't fit flush at the shoulders. You can correct this by removing the screws on the jig parts, realigning them, and screwing them back down. But if you very carefully align them to begin with, you can get the alignment close enough for accurate joinery.

Begin making the jig by cutting out the three plywood pieces that make the base, the carrier base and the vertical carrier face. Make the base from ³⁄₄"-thick plywood, so it's thick enough to take a hanger bolt well. Bore ⁵⁄₁₆" holes in the carrier base along the line of the slot for the securing bolt as shown in the drawing. Then use a chisel to clean up the sides of the slot. Center the slot along the width of the base.

Get out the three perimeter pieces that will attach to the base, and install a T-nut in the rear piece. Center it along the length, but make it a bit higher than center along the width of the piece so the bolt won't hit the plywood of the carrier base. Screw one of the two side perimeter pieces, as well as the rear piece, to the base with the T-nut. Place the carrier base against the first side perimeter piece. Clamp the other in place, so that the carrier base can slide back and forth between the two without any slop. Screw the third

*This scaled-down version of the more complicated tenoning jig shown previously takes little time to make and produces accurate mortise and tenon joints.*

perimeter piece down.

Make the triangular supports for the vertical carrier face out of solid stock, which takes screws better than plywood. Cut them out on the table saw using the miter gauge set at 45°. Start with a piece at least 30" long so you have plenty to grip on the miter gauge for safety. Orient the grain of the parts parallel to the diagonal side of the triangles. The combination of two 45° cuts for each triangle should yield a 90° angle between the horizontal and vertical edges of the parts. Be sure this is 90°. If it is not, adjust the edges

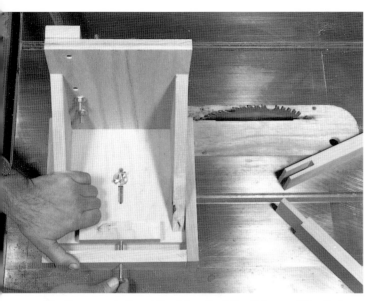

*The jig uses a bolt and T-nut to adjust the distance of the jig face from the saw blade, and another to secure the adjustment in place.*

with a stationary sander, but don't try using the table saw, because now they are too short.

Screw together all five of the carrier pieces. Set the triangles in from the edge of the carrier base slightly so that they do not contact the base side pieces and cause the carrier to bind. Place the carrier in the base, and mark a location on the base through the slot for the securing bolt. Remove the carrier, and bore a hole in the base for a hanger bolt and wing nut, which secure the carrier to the base. When you screw down the hanger bolt, don't screw it through the bottom of the plywood.

Make a runner that fits in the miter gauge groove of your table saw. Where you screw this piece to the bottom of the base determines the range of distance from the blade that the jig will handle. Determine your needs, and clamp the runner to the jig parallel to the vertical carrier face, then screw it down. Follow the instructions at the end of chapter three for making mortises and tenons with a tenoning jig.

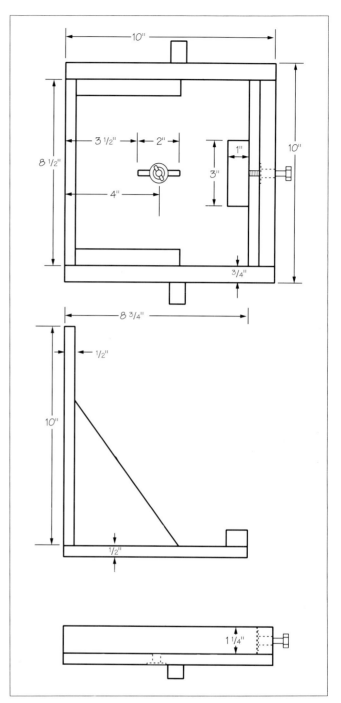

*The jig at top consists of two main parts: a base (at bottom) and a carrier (center) that fits within the base.*

# 8 TABLE SAW CUTOFF BOXES

*Use this cutoff box on your table saw to make accurate crosscuts on your stock.*

The easiest way to cut pieces to length is with a radial arm saw mounted against the wall with tables built on either side to support the work. These cutoff boxes on the table saw are the next best thing. These cutoff boxes are more accurate than a miter gauge because they provide more support for the part as it is cut. If you like, make one box for right-angle cutoffs, and another for miters as shown in the photos.

Begin these boxes with pieces of plywood at least 30" square. Screw thick, wide pieces of solid stock to the back of each piece of plywood, and to the front of the right-angle cutoff box. These pieces give you a large area to grip, and must be tall where the blade

passes through them leaving enough wood above the cut so that the piece is still strong. Make wooden runners that will fit into the miter gauge grooves on your table saw, and screw these to the bottom of the plywood. On the right-angle cutoff box, these runners must be located at exactly 90° to the rear fence in order for cuts made on the box to be at exactly 90°.

Many projects will require you to cut a number of pieces at the same length. This is easy to do with an end stop attached to whatever cutoff arrangement you use. To mount such an end stop on this right-angle cutoff box, cut a ¾"×¾" groove in the back of the rear fence, at 1" above the bottom of the fence. Screw to this groove an extension piece that extends left of the blade farther than the longest piece that you need to cut. Make an end stop that clamps to the extension piece, as shown in the photos, and that can slide along the extension piece for adjustment. To make minute adjustments of the end stop, loosen its clamp so that it still holds the part in place, but with minimal pressure. Then gently tap it in the direction you want, and tighten the clamp again. Attach extensions of any length you need for your parts.

For cutting miters, make a special box as shown or just attach 45° miter fences to your right-angle box. There are two approaches to getting accurate miter joints with such a box. The first is to carefully locate the miter fence so that it is exactly 45° to the blade. The second is to locate one fence on one side of the blade as close as you can to 45°. Then attach another fence on the other side of the blade, and locate this at exactly 90° to the first fence. Make one side of your miter cuts on the left fence, and the other side on the right fence. Even if the angle cut is not exactly 45°, the joint ends up at 90° because the second cut is away from 45° the same amount as the first—but in the other direction.

**Attach an extension arm and stop block to the back of your 90° cutoff box to cut parts to length in repeatable sizes.**

**To cut miters, build a separate box with 45° fences or attach fences to your 90° box. The care you take in placing the fences will determine the fit of the miter joints.**

# 9 | USING A DADO CUTTER

A dado cutter is a special blade for the table saw that cuts wider kerfs than a regular combination or rip blade. There are two basic designs for dado cutters— stacking and wobble. A stacking set has two blades that make the edges of the cut, and chip breakers that go between them to clear the waste. With this type you adjust the cut width by stacking more or fewer chip breakers between the outer blades. The wobble type has one blade mounted on beveled plates. By shifting the relation between these plates, the amount of wobble on the blade is lessened or increased, respectively lessening or increasing the width of the cut. The one disadvantage to the wobble type is that at wider settings, the bottom of the cut is not flat but arced at the radius of the cutter itself. Stacking cutters always produce a flat bottom.

You'll need special inserts for your table saw top to accommodate the extra wide cutter. Make these out of plywood on a router table with a bearing-guided flush trim bit. Attach your old insert to the plywood and flush trim it to the contour of the old one. Raise the spinning dado cutter through the new insert to cut a hole for it. When you do this, hold the insert down with a pushstick. Don't hold it down with your hand!

Cutting a groove in the middle of a board is a very simple procedure. Set your cutter at the width of cut you want, and reference the cut to the rip fence as in photo 1. Set the depth of cut by the height of the cutter.

On the other hand, cutting a rabbet in the edge of a board presents a problem since the cutter must come up against the edge of the rip fence. To avoid cutting up your rip fence, attach an auxiliary fence to it as in photo 2. You won't mind cutting into this. Set the dado cutter at a width greater than the rabbet you want to cut. Lower the cutter below the table. Attach the auxiliary fence, and slide it over the cutter. Don't slide it so far that the rip fence itself is over the cutter. Turn on the saw and raise the cutter into the auxiliary fence to a height just beyond the rabbet depth you want.

Now turn off the saw, and move the rip fence away

Photo 1—Cut a groove in the face or edge of a part with a dado cutter in the table saw. Use the rip fence to establish the distance of the groove from the part edge.

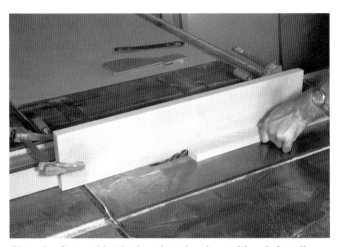

Photo 2—Cut a rabbet in the edge of a piece with a dado cutter and an auxiliary fence attached to the rip fence. Raise the blade into the auxiliary fence so it doesn't cut the rip fence itself.

from the blade until you arrive at the correct rabbet width. Set the cutter height for your depth, and you're ready. If you want to run the parts on edge, the clamps will get in the way. In this case, screw the auxiliary fence to the rip fence, burying the heads with countersinks.

Last but not least—never run your fingers over the cutter, even when it is completely covered by the work.

# 10 PLUNGE ROUTER MORTISING JIG

This jig cuts closed or "blind" mortises anywhere along the edge of parts. There are significant differences between these and the open mortises cut by the table saw tenoning jigs (chapters three and seven). Closed mortises are hidden from view and produce a very different aesthetic effect. Open mortises depend entirely on the glue bond for their strength, whereas a tenon tightly enclosed in a blind mortise is mechanically strong so long as it stays in the mortise. And of course, you can't cut an open mortise in the middle of a piece.

The plunge router mortising jig is designed to make cutting closed mortises fast and easy. Once it is set up, loading and unloading parts into and out of the jig is quick, and its stable design ensures that the cuts will be well aligned. Fairly fast to set up, this jig is efficient to use even when cutting just a few mortises. The one major drawback to plunge routing mortises is that the ends of the mortise are left round by the bit. This requires that you either square up the ends with a chisel or round the tenons to match. This is the trade off for very speedy and accurate holes.

Use a plunge router only with this jig. It won't work well at all with a fixed router base, and attempts to do so will be dangerous. If you don't have a plunge router, either get one or do your mortising by

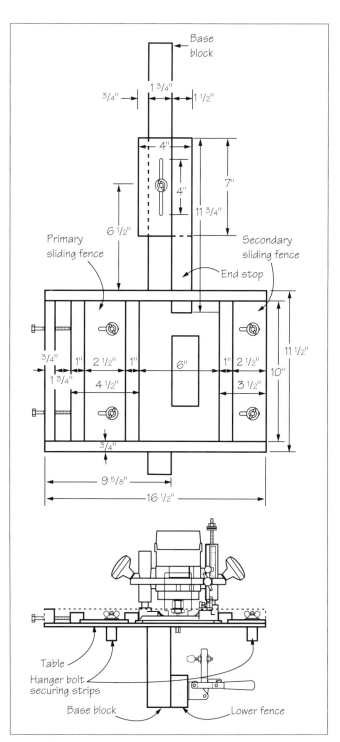

The two main components of the plunge router mortising jig are the base block, which the work is clamped to, and the table on which the router rides.

## MATERIALS LIST

| Part | | Dimension |
|------|--|-----------|
| A | Plywood table | ¼" × 11½" × 16½" |
| B | Plywood fence | ¼" × 4½" × 10" |
| C | Plywood fence | ¼" × 3½" × 10" |
| D | Plywood end stop | ¼" × 4" × 7" |
| E | Table sides (2) | ¾" × 1" × 16½" |
| F | Fences and table end (4) | ¾" × 1" × 10" |
| G | Hanger bolt securing strips (2) | ¾" × 1" × 11½" |
| H | End stop | ½" × 1½" × 11¾" |
| I | End stop fence | ¾" × ¾" × 7" |
| J | Base block | 1¾" × 6" × 30" |

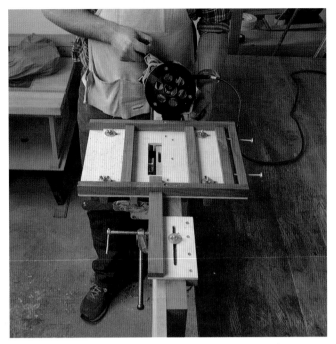

*This plunge router mortising jig is designed to cut mortises very quickly. You load your parts below the jig table with a toggle clamp, and cut down into the part from above with the router.*

*You can cut clean rounded mortises using the plunge router mortising jig.*

other means.

The components of the jig break into two major areas: above the table and below. The table is the rectangular piece of plywood that your plunge router sits on, and everything above the table functions to align the plunge router and limit its travel. The components below the table align the workpiece. The two areas are combined with one large piece, the base block, to which the table is attached and the lower fence gets clamped. You clamp the workpiece to the base block, and the cut is referenced to the base block face.

The components above the table must do two jobs. First they must align the mortise along the part width accurately. Center the mortise or locate it off center. Secondly, the jig must limit the length of the cut.

Two sliding fences on top of the table align the router base to the width of your part. The jig uses bolts and metal-threaded inserts to fine-tune this adjustment. Once this is set, clamp both fences down firmly to the table with wing nuts. The length of mortise you cut is determined by how far to the left or right you can slide the plunge router within the two base fences. On one side of the jig the base will butt against the side of the jig itself; on the other side it hits an adjustable end stop.

Finally, the depth of cut is set with the plunge router adjustments, and the mortise width by the bit itself.

Begin the jig by cutting to length and width the

plywood pieces for the table, two fences and end stop. Mark out on these pieces the locations of the slots for the hanger bolts, as well as the central hole in the table. Bore 5/16" holes along the slot lines on the fences and end stop as in photo 1 (page 27). Also bore four holes at the corners of the table hole. Use a scroll or saber saw to finish the slots and cut out the table hole as in photo 2 (page 27).

Get out the ten hardwood pieces that attach to the table, fences and end stop plywood rectangles. Install two threaded inserts in the rear table piece as shown in photo 3 (page 28). Clamp this piece in place on the table, and secure it with screws.

Attach two of the hardwood pieces beneath the table as shown in the drawing. The sole purpose of these two pieces is to provide wood for the hanger bolts to screw into. To screw down a hanger bolt, put a wing nut onto it, and thread the wing nut to the base of the bolt threads until it stops. Then use a wrench on the wing nut to turn the hanger bolt into the hole as in photo 4 (page 28). The holes you drill for the hanger bolts should be large enough not to cause a lot of resistance as the bolt is screwed down. Once the bolt is in place, loosen the wing nut with a sharp rap from a hammer.

Cut rabbets in the hardwood pieces for the two fences as shown in the drawing. The depth of the rabbets depends on the thickness of your plywood. Cut a smaller rabbet along the edges of these pieces that contact the router base. This gives the router

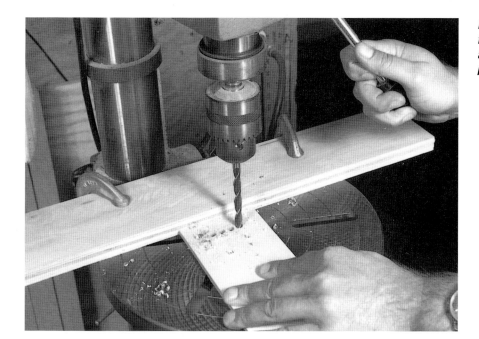

*Photo 1—Bore holes in the plywood table, fences and end stop for the mortising area and hanger bolt slots. Set up on the drill press to accurately locate the holes.*

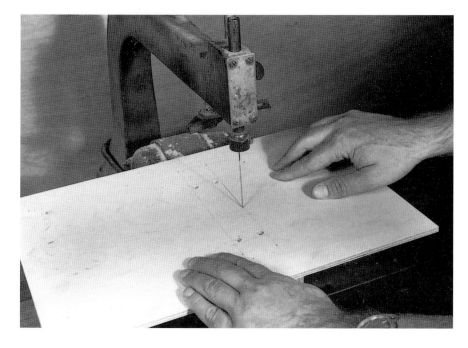

*Photo 2—Clear out the waste within the holes with a scroll saw or saber saw.*

chips somewhere to go as the base pushes them against the fences. This rabbet cannot be so high that the edge of your router base falls into it. Screw these pieces to the plywood fences.

Clamp the table in place on the base block and screw it down. Make sure that the rear hardwood strip is parallel to the base block. This will help you align the fence when you adjust it.

Screw the two end stop hardwood pieces to the end stop plywood. Then put the end stop on the base block and slide it toward the table until it passes over the table. Place one of the edge pieces over the stop, and mark where the two overlap. Remove the edge piece and cut out a hole here for the end stop to fit

through, using a handsaw and chisels. Attach both edge pieces with screws. Put the end stop in place, mark the location for the end stop hanger bolt through the slot in the plywood, and install the hanger bolt.

Attach two boards to the back of the base piece, so that you can clamp the jig into a vise. Now clamp a bottom fence onto the base block. The bottom fence is just a piece of stock about 3/4"×3"×24". Vary the size of this fence according to the size of parts that you put into the jig. Clamp the fence below the table at a distance just over the width of the parts you intend to mortise as in photo 5 (page 29). Then attach two toggle clamps to this fence on either side of the hole in the table. One toggle clamp is not

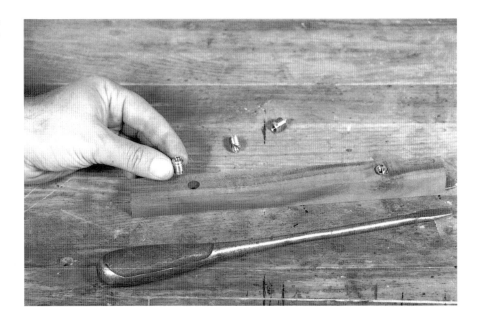

*Photo 3—Install threaded inserts into the rear table piece. These metal inserts will hold the bolts that adjust the position of the primary fence on the jig table.*

*Photo 4—Install hanger bolts through the table into the securing strips beneath. Be careful to bore holes that are wide enough to allow the hanger bolts to be installed without too much effort, but not so wide that they are loose.*

enough to guarantee that the parts will lie flat on the base block. Don't place the toggle clamps directly over a mortise, or they will push in the walls.

Now put a test piece in the jig and clamp it down with the toggle clamps. Locate the primary fence so that the router bit will be approximately on center to the part. Make a test cut, and see how far off center it is. Use the adjustment bolts on the primary fence to move it to the correct direction. The rear hardwood strip is parallel to the base block. Therefore, when the fence is parallel to the rear strip, it follows that the fence must also be parallel to the base block. Measure carefully as you adjust the fence to keep it parallel to the rear strip.

Once the primary fence is correctly aligned, set the secondary fence in place parallel to it so that the

router base slides tightly between them. Now adjust the end stop. Butt the router base against the side strip opposite the end stop, as in photo 6 (page 29). Use a measuring stick to determine the distance from the router base to the end stop. Make this distance equal to the length of mortise you want, minus the width of the router bit you are using. Secure the end stop down.

How far do you want your mortise to be from the end of the part? Establish this distance with an end stop clamped onto the bottom fence, as shown in photo 5 (page 29). Cut each mortise in stages, plunging down about ¼" on each pass. One thing to watch for is accumulated router chips. Clear them away so they don't impede the travel of the router.

Photo 5—Clamp a fence to the base block with C-clamps. Attach toggle clamps to this fence. Clamp an end stop to the fence to locate the mortises along the length of your parts.

Photo 6—Set the length of the mortise by adjusting the end stop. Slide a steel rule over the top of the stop itself until it hits the router base.

# 11 MAKING DOVETAILS WITH A ROUTER TABLE

This setup for the router table lets you make variably spaced through dovetails with only two router bits and a simple shop-made jig. The method is faster than cutting dovetails by hand, but not as fast as using most of the store-bought jigs described later in the book. Also, this method is not as precise as using store-bought jigs, and it requires you to make very careful adjust-

*You can make variably spaced through dovetails on your router table with this simple jig. The small dovetail on top of the jig serves as the reference point that lets you align the dovetails to their corresponding pins.*

ments to fit the joints together. Once you get this procedure down, however, you can make tight, consistent joints in a reasonable amount of time.

There are two parts to a dovetail joint: the dovetails and the pins. The dovetails are very easy to cut at a router table with a dovetail bit and a vertical fence, as in photo 2 (page 32). The trick is to cut pins that fit tightly between the dovetails. Setting up the angles to cut the pins is easy enough to do, but how do you accurately space the pins to match the tails?

Recall the introduction to this section, where I spoke about three factors for building jigs: *alignment*, *reference* and *adjustability*. With this jig the dovetail bit and jig will align the angles of the cuts. But to space the pins to match the tails, you need a point of reference that shows where the pins must be in order to fit. And, you must be able to adjust this point of reference so you can adjust the fit of the joint. With this setup you use the face of each dovetail as a reference point to locate the face of the adjoining pin. You make adjustments to the fit of the joint by moving that reference point along a sliding fence.

Start by making the jig itself, which consists of three layers. Make all three layers at least 4" wide so that as you cut parts on the router table you can keep your fingers away from the bit. First make layer one as shown in the drawing with a pair of 2" long slots for hanger bolts. Attach this layer to your miter gauge.

With layer one attached to the miter gauge, set the gauge at 90° and install your dovetail bit in the table at a height of 7/16". Now cut a dovetail into the end of a piece of stock as in photo 1 (page 32). Make this

**All you need to make dovetails on your router table are two bits and the jig described in this chapter.**

dovetail smaller in width than the width of the dovetail bit. Then use a handsaw to cut away the ends on either side of the dovetail, so it alone extends beyond the end of the piece. Now cut this piece to length at the width of your layers. Measure this length from the base of the dovetail, not the top of it.

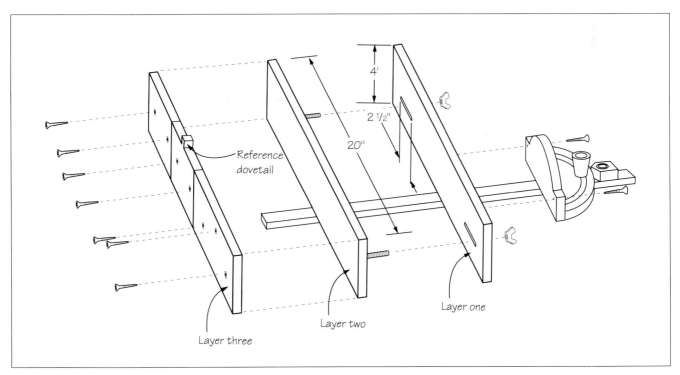

**The router table dovetail jig consists of your miter gauge and three wooden layers assembled as shown.**

Photo 1—Make a dovetail reference pin for the jig by cutting out a small dovetail on the end of a board as shown. Cut off the end pieces with a hand saw, leaving the center dovetail.

Photo 2—Cut dovetails on the ends of your parts with the same setup as the previous photo. Space the dovetails as you like. Be sure the part does not slide around during the cut.

Photo 3—Mark out the tails by placing the pin boards on end on the dovetails and scribing with a razor blade where the dovetail ends hit the pin boards.

This small dovetail becomes the reference point for aligning the pins. Screw the piece with the dovetail to layer number two. Position the dovetail so it is centered over the bit when the ends of all three layers are flush. Attach filler pieces on either side. Don't place any screws in the area of the bit—you don't want to hit screws while making cuts.

Use a dovetail bit with an angle of between 8° and 12°. Much more or less than that will provide a weaker joint. Note that the height of your dovetail bit limits the thickness of the parts you can use.

Attach layers two and three to layer one with hanger bolts that fit within the slots in layer one. Locate the bolts at the center of each of the slots when the reference dovetail is centered over the bit.

Prepare your stock that will get the dovetails. I suggest that you first use test pieces to learn how the jig works before cutting parts for a project. It is very important with this setup that your parts be ripped to exactly the same width, and cut off at exactly 90° on the ends. If the ends are not 90°, they will sit on the jig at an odd angle, which will affect the alignment of the pins.

Begin cutting joints by removing layers two and three from the jig, and setting the miter gauge at 90°. Put the dovetail bit in the router table, and set its height above the table at the thickness of your stock. Now cut the dovetails into the ends of parts that get them, as in photo 2. Space the dovetails as you wish. Traditionally, the ends of dovetail joints are taken up by half pins rather than half dovetails. Be sure to cut enough off the ends of your pieces so that the pins will be at least 1/4" thick for strength.

Be sure that the piece does not slide to the right or left along the fence during the cut. If you think the part may have moved, make a second pass on suspect faces to ensure that the cut is straight. You don't need to position the dovetails uniformly from piece to piece. Since the pins for each joint will be positioned by using the very tails that the pins will contact, the tails can be randomly located from joint to joint.

Now take each dovetailed end and place it on the bench, dovetails toward you and the inside of the piece up, as in photo 3. Place the corresponding part that will get pins on the dovetails as shown, inside away from you, and mark the position of the dovetail ends on the outer edge of the pin piece with a razor blade. Make pencil marks above the razor lines so you can find them. Make an × in each area that will be cut away between pins. Now lay the pin piece flat on the dovetail piece so the inside faces of each make contact. Leave them momentarily.

Attach layers two and three to the jig with the hanger bolts. Lift the two pieces off the bench and place them on the jig as in photo 4. Let the pin piece slide until it hits the router table. Line up the two edges of the parts exactly, and clamp them together with clamp blocks and C-clamps as shown. It is important that the edges are flush, and that the ends of the pin and dovetailed pieces rest flat on the table and jig respectively.

Place a straight flute bit in the router table and raise it to the thickness of your stock. Tilt the miter gauge counterclockwise the same number of degrees as your dovetail bit. The jig is now aligned to cut the pin faces that are on the left of each pin, seen as you stand behind the jig as in photo 5. Push the clamped pieces to the right so that one right edge of a dovetail hits the reference dovetail on the jig. Loosen the wing nuts on the hanger bolts and slide the second and third jig layers along until the bit aligns with the razor mark for a left pin face. Align the bit to cut the pin face that will contact the dovetail face, which is presently hitting the dovetail reference piece.

Align the jig so that the bit cuts just beyond the razor mark by about 1/16". Tighten the wing nuts and cut all the left pin faces on this piece. Check to see how close they all are to the razor marks, then adjust the jig to make the cuts right to the razor lines. Do so by loosening the wing nuts and gently tapping layer two of the jig and watching to see how far it moves in relation to layer one. Make the cuts again. Continue to adjust and cut until the cuts split the razor lines. When this is correctly aligned, cut all the left pin faces for your joints.

Next tilt the miter gauge clockwise to cut the opposite faces of the pins. To cut the right pin faces, push the clamped parts to the left against the dovetail reference piece. First adjust the jig to cut the pins too large, then gradually move the jig in to bring the pins to size. Between cuts remove the clamps from the pieces and test fit the joint. When you reassemble the clamped pieces, be sure to put them back exactly as they were.

When you have adjusted the jig to cut one of the joints tightly, the jig should cut all the rest of your joints tightly too. But this will only be true if all the other cuts you made were consistent. At first, do separate setups for each joint for the second pin face cuts. Reset the jig between joints to cut the pins too large at first, and gradually make them smaller as described above. After you gain confidence with the jig and its operation, try using one secondary pin face setup to cut multiple joints.

**Photo 4**—Place the dovetail and pin boards together—insides touching—and clamp them together. Rest the end of the dovetail board on the jig, and the end of the tail board on the router table.

**Photo 5**—Tilt the miter gauge counterclockwise the same number of degrees as your router bit. Push one of the dovetails on the dovetail board against the dovetail reference piece, and adjust the jig so that the pin face will contact that dovetail.

**Photo 6**—Cut the opposite side of each pin by turning the miter gauge clockwise and duplicating the process. When you are finished, unclamp the parts and cut out waste between the pins by holding the part on the jig located by eye.

# 12 ROUTER TENONING JIG

I n previous chapters we looked at several ways to cut tenons, including using a table saw tenoning jig and using a dado cutter and the miter fence as a guide. This chapter shows another way to skin the same cat, and it has several advantages over the other methods. This technique makes clean, accurate tenons in one step, whereas the table saw tenoning jig requires two steps to get a clean shoulder on the tenon. While cutting tenons on the table saw with a dado cutter and miter fence can be done in only one step, it is the least accurate of the three methods and likely to produce some tearout where it will be visible.

To understand how this jig works, look at the circled drawing showing a cross section of the router base, jig table and workpiece. The jig holds a straight flute bit at a certain distance from the vertical face of the jig by means of a router template guide that hits the jig's top table edge. You clamp your workpiece to the vertical face of the jig with a toggle clamp, then push your router along the top table of the jig as shown in the photo with the template guide rubbing against the edge of the table. In the process the bit cuts one side of the tenon, cutting both the face and shoulder in one pass. Then you flip the part and cut the other side to complete the tenon.

Notice there are several factors here that determine exactly how thick the tenon will be. The first is the distance of the jig's top table edge from the vertical face of the jig. The second is the distance between the edge of the template guide and the edge of the bit. The last factor is the thickness of the part being cut.

First build the jig as shown, but don't yet screw down the top table. The dimensions of the jig aren't critical; it just needs to hold the top table at 90° to the vertical face, and the edges of the side fences against which the parts will lie must also be at 90° to the top face. Other than that, just screw your pieces together well so it will be sturdy and safe, and adjust the dimensions so that it will be at a comfortable working height above your bench.

Now get out your template guides and straight flute bits. Find the smallest diameter guide and largest diameter bit that will fit through the guide. Look at

*This router tenoning jig lets you make many accurate tenons in very little time.*

the drawing, and you will see that the end of the tenon hits the bottom of the top table. If your template guide were a lot wider, you would have to locate the top table so far back that the end of the tenon would not touch it. It must touch to establish the accurate length of the tenon. Say you use a ⅝" guide and a ⅜" bit, the distance between the two would be ⅛" (or half of ⅝ minus ⅜).

How thick is your stock, and how thick do you want your tenon to be? Common practice with mortise and tenon joints is to make the tenon one-third the thickness of the parts, so with ¾"-thick stock you might use a ¼" tenon. In this case, the router bit must be ½" from the vertical face of the jig when the cut is made. With the ⅝" guide and ⅜" bit described above, you would have to locate the top table edge at ⅜" from the vertical face to achieve this. Clamp the top table in place at this distance, carefully measuring with a steel rule, then screw it down.

Anyone who has used template guides at all knows that they usually aren't perfectly centered to the bit. So on one side of the router base the distance from the edge of the guide to the bit, with the above combination, will be a fraction over ⅛", and on the other side it will be a fraction less. Use this difference to your advantage. Make tests holding the router in different positions, and see which position makes a thicker tenon and which makes a thinner one. When you cut the parts, you'll know just where to hold the router to get the right thickness to match your mortises.

Be careful as you make these cuts. Don't try to make tenons longer than 1½", otherwise the bit would protrude so far as to be very dangerous. Even with small tenons, there is a danger, so watch that bit! Don't try to make the whole cut in one pass. Cut only about 1/16" deep with each stroke.

*The jig holds stock in place with a toggle clamp, and the router rides on the table top. A template guide in the router base rubs against the leading edge of the table.*

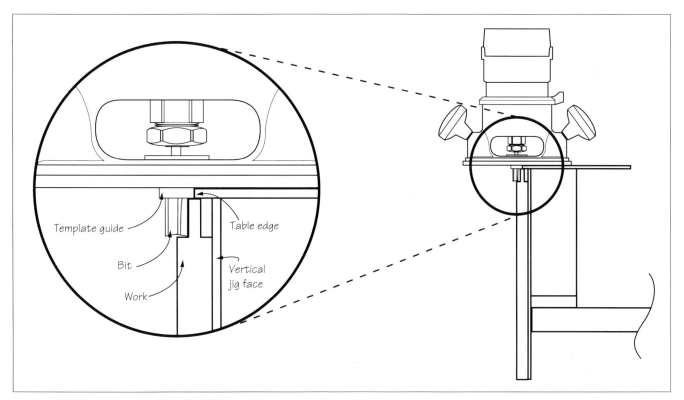

Template guide

Table edge

Bit

Vertical jig face

Work

*The thickness of the tenon is determined by the distance between the bit and the template guide, the distance between the edge of the table and the vertical jig face, and the thickness of your work.*

# 13 MAKING ROUTER TEMPLATES

**W**ith a template guide mounted in your router base and a template of your chosen dimensions, you can quickly cut uniform and neat mortises for hinges or for joining wooden parts. A template guide is a metal ring that mounts in your router base, with a circular collar that protrudes below the base by ½" or less. You mount a straight flute bit in the router collet. The bit fits through the center of the guide ring. You push the guide ring against the edge of a template, and the bit cuts the wood beneath the template, following its pattern as in the photo at right.

You can make a template of any pattern you like. If the pattern you want is simple and you need to cut many pieces (like the drawer guides for the bench cabinets in chapter nineteen), then the small amount of time you spend making the template is very worthwhile. Once you have a template, you can cut out patterns quickly. The method I describe here is for making templates that cut square mortises. These templates are quick and easy to make, so they are worthwhile if you plan to cut more than three or four mortises. If you only have one or two to cut, do them with chisels.

Before you begin making your template, you must decide which template guide and bit you will use. This is critical, because you will make the template to match the sizes of the two. Say you want a drawer guide mortise that is ¾" wide, and you have a ½" template guide and ¼" bit. The edge of the template guide will be ⅛" away from the edge of the bit all the way around the bit. See the photo above. Therefore, the actual size of the template must be ⅛" larger than the size of the intended mortise along each side of the mortise. The template for the ¾" drawer guide must be 1" wide so that the resulting mortise will be ¾" wide. However, where you place the template on the wood determines the length of the mortise (since one end of the mortise along its length is open).

Once you have figured the width of your template, use 1× stock to make setup pieces for the template. Rip one setup piece to exactly the width you desire for the template width. Then, nest this piece between

**Photo 1—A template and template guide are used to cut drawer guide mortises similar to those on the bench cabinets shown in chapter nineteen.**

two wider pieces (at least 3" wide) as shown in photo 2 (page 37).

Clamp the three setup pieces together as shown in photo 3 (page 37). Use them to trace the U shape they make onto a piece of template plywood, then rough cut the waste from within that tracing with a saber, band or scroll saw. Make these rough cuts within the traced lines. Place the plywood on the setup pieces as shown in photo 3, then nail the plywood to the setup pieces with two or three small finish nails.

Use a bearing-guided flush trim bit in your router to flush trim the plywood to the shape of the setup pieces beneath as in photo 4 (page 37). Clamp the entire assembly to your bench to prevent it from moving as you flush trim. Next remove the template from the setup pieces and remove the nails. You're through with the setup pieces now.

Next attach a fence onto the bottom of the template to limit the length of the mortise. The width of the mortise is established by the distance between the two sides of the template; the length is established by how far the end of the template U is located from the edge of the part that gets the mortise. The fence you

Photo 2—Set up to make your template by sandwiching three setup pieces together as shown. The center piece should be the same width as the template you desire.

Photo 3—Clamp the three together, then use them to trace a U shape onto a piece of plywood. Cut out the waste within the U.

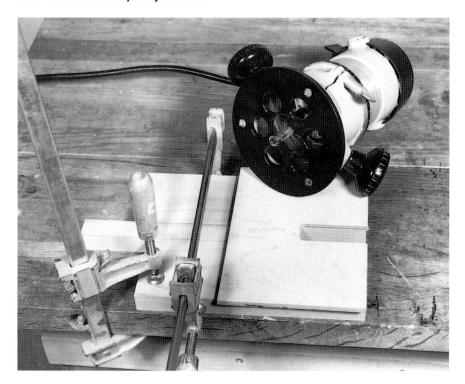

Photo 4—Nail the plywood to the setup pieces and use a bearing-guided flush trim bit to flush trim the template to the size of the U in the setup pieces. The template is finished except for attaching a fence, which locates it on the work (see photo 1).

attach to the template butts against one edge of the part, and so establishes the mortise length. If you want a mortise length of $1\frac{1}{2}$", place the fence from the end of the template U at $1\frac{1}{2}$" plus the difference between bit and guide, as discussed above. In this case, the distance from the fence to the end of the U would be $1\frac{5}{8}$". Nail the fence to the plywood with six or eight small finish nails.

Set up to cut a mortise as shown in photo 1 (page 34). Clamp the piece that gets the mortise onto your bench edge. Place the template on the piece with the fence butted against one edge. Align it properly side to side, and clamp it to the part. Set up the router with the template guide and bit. Note that the depth

of the mortise is determined by the depth adjustment on the router base. Make tests to get the correct depth.

Notice that when you cut the mortise, you will cut into the top of the template fence. This is fine so long as you don't cut all the way through. You could also attach the fence to the other side of the template or anywhere, provided the template is held in the correct location.

You may need to cut your template guides shorter with a hack saw to accommodate the thickness of your plywood. The guide cannot protrude beyond the base farther than the thickness of the plywood.

# 14 ROUTER RADIUSING JIG

*This router radiusing jig lets you make circular templates for flush trimming the edges of curved furniture parts.*

Putting curves in your woodworking gives you a lot of attractive design possibilities. Even a single, simple curve can make a world of difference on an otherwise rectangular cabinet. Look ahead to chapter twenty-three on building wall-mounted storage cabinets, and notice the curved top rails on the doors. It would be easier to make straight top rails—but the curves make the cabinets look much better. You'll make those top rails using a template made with this router radiusing jig.

The purpose of this jig is to attach the router to a pivot point around which it turns. Pivoting along this

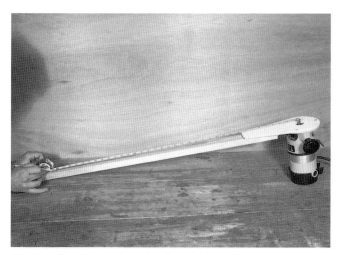

Photo 1—*The jig consists of a plywood base that screws to your router base. Attached to that base is a short connector piece to which you can screw extension pieces of any length, depending on the radius you need to cut.*

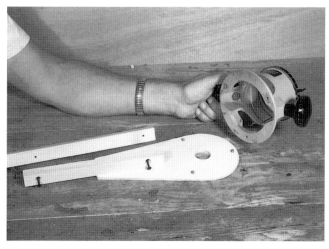

Photo 2—*Locate a pivot hole on the extension piece by measuring from the bit to the correct location on the extension. Measure from the outside of the bit for internal curves, and from the inside for external curves.*

reference point, the router cuts an arc of that specific radius. You could use this setup to cut out parts for projects, but it isn't all that easy to cut through thick parts with this setup. For that reason it is best to use this jig to make curved templates out of ¼" or ½" plywood, then use the templates to make parts by flush trimming on a router table.

First make a plywood sub-base for your router as shown in photo 1. Trace the basic shape from the router base itself, marking the screw holes. Then draw a triangular extension about 10" away from the base as shown. Cut out the base with a band, scroll or saber saw, and cut out the center. Drill the screw holes for the base and countersink them far enough so the screw heads will not protrude beyond the face of the plywood.

Next screw a piece about ¾"×¾"×12" onto the base as shown. To this piece you can then attach any length extension you need to get whatever radius you require.

Say you need to cut a curved template of 3' in radius. Attach an extension onto the base that is just over 3'. Next, screw the jig base onto your router base, and put a straight flute carbide bit into the router motor. Mount the motor in the base, and flip it over as in photo 2.

Now comes the tricky part. Do you need to cut an internal or external radius? The curve on the doors of the wall-mounted cabinets (chapter twenty-three) is an internal radius, and the template used to make this curve is cut with the outside of the router bit. That is, when you make the arcing cut through the plywood, you get two templates—one on the inside of the bit

closest to the pivot point, and one on the outside of the bit away from the pivot point. For those cabinet doors, you use the outside template, which has a concave, or internal radius. If you wanted to make the top of the door curved, with a curve that parallels the existing one, that curve would be convex, or external, and would be made using a template cut by the inside of the bit, closest to the pivot point.

Because an internal curve is cut by the outside of the router bit, measure from the outside of the bit when you position the pivot point hole as in photo 2. For an external radius, you need to measure from the inside of the bit. Mark the extension, and bore a hole there for a nail or screw to serve as the actual pivot. The hole should be slightly less than the diameter of the pivot so the nail or screw won't be loose.

Use a large piece of low-grade plywood as a base for cutting the template. Secure the template stock on top of the base plywood with small nails, but be sure to place them away from the area to be cut. Sink the pivot nail or screw into the base plywood at a location that allows the router to swing over the template stock where you want it. Set the depth of cut to just beyond the depth of the template plywood, and cut out the arc.

Be sure to secure both sides of the template stock to the base plywood so that when the cut is complete you don't have a loose piece of plywood cut free. This could get caught by the bit and thrown. Use a carbide straight flute bit to cut plywood—plywood has a lot of glue and carbide cuts through glue. A steel bit would dull in a hurry.

# 15 MORE JIGS AND FIXTURES

Cutting a full sheet of plywood.

## Handling Large Sheets of Plywood

Unless you have large extension tables on your table saw, cutting a whole sheet of plywood can be difficult. But once you make the first cut in the sheet, the pieces are usually small enough to handle on any table saw. Make those initial cuts by setting up on sawhorses as shown in the photo. Place long pieces of scrap stock or three 8' studs across the horses and put the plywood on top of them. Mark where you want your cut. Clamp a straightedge fence onto the plywood as shown. Adjust the fence away from your marked line the same distance that the blade on your circular saw is from the edge of its base. Run the saw base along the edge of the fence. Set the depth of cut on the saw to just beyond the thickness of the

plywood, so that the blade barely cuts into the support pieces below them.

When you cut plywood on the table saw, keep the edge of the plywood firmly against the saw fence, and hold the plywood down firmly so that it does not raise above the blade. If the plywood does raise up and get on top of the blade, the blade can throw the plywood.

## Tilt Table for the Drill Press

Use this jig to bore holes at accurate angles other than 90°. Make the jig out of two pieces of ¾" plywood attached at one end with two hinges. Make the

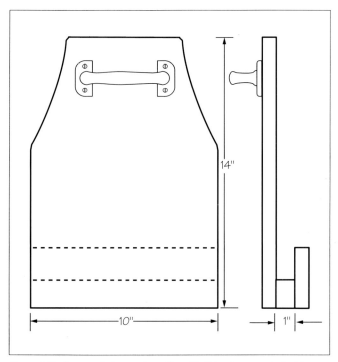

*Carry full sheets of plywood easily with this shop-made holder.*

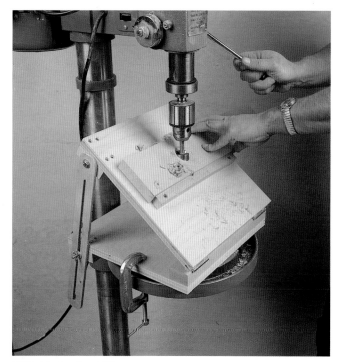

*Tilt table for the drill press.*

sliding supports out of ¼" Baltic birch plywood, or a similar good quality plywood. A cheaper plywood will not hold up well and will invariably splinter and break.

To make the long slot in the sliding supports, set up the router table with a ⁵⁄₁₆" straight flute bit and a straight fence set at ¾" from the center of the bit. Mark on the plywood the location of the long slot. Facing the router table with the bit between you and the fence, lower the plywood onto the cutter at the left side of the slot. Push the plywood along the fence to the opposite end. Don't pass your fingers by the bit. Use a 3'-long piece of plywood so you can keep your fingers away. Cut the piece shorter after cutting the slots.

When you push the piece in this direction, the bit tends to push the work toward the fence rather than away. If you start at the other end and push the opposite way, the bit will pull the plywood away.

Attach blocks as shown in the photo for the pivot bolts and the hanger bolts that protrude through the support slots. Put wing nuts on the hanger bolts. The wing nuts are strong enough to hold the jig at the angle you set for most boring jobs. If you have to really bear down on it, put a support block under the tilting table to take some of the force. Attach whatever fences you need to the table to support parts being bored so they won't slide down.

The best kind of bit to use for boring angled holes is a Forstner bit, which can enter a hole at an angle without deflecting. But these bits have poor chip

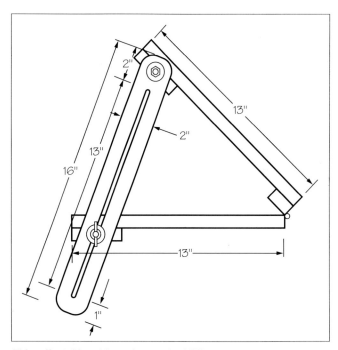

*This adjustable table makes angle drilling easy.*

clearance, so remember to lift the bit out every ½" or so to clear the chips, or you'll get the bit stuck in the hole.

## Folding Extension Tables for Machines

In a large shop, permanent tables alongside machines are very handy for long stock to ride on as it is cut. But in a small shop where space is tight, you can

*Extension table raised.*

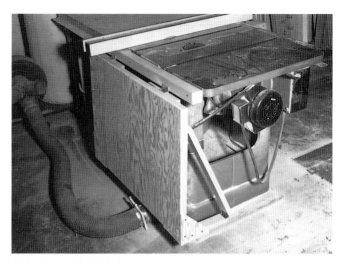

*Extension table folded.*

install an extension table that folds down when not in use. Build the table itself out of any available plywood. Construct a perimeter beneath it of solid stock for stiffness and for screwing the hinges and legs to. If you want, join the corners of the perimeter pieces with open mortise and tenon joints as shown in chapter two. Screw the plywood securely to the perimeter pieces.

Attach a piece of wood to the edge of the machine table that contacts the extension table, so that you can screw the hinges into wood. Bore two bolt holes in the table edge to hold the piece of wood. Once it is in place, you have a base onto which you can locate and relocate hinges as necessary.

Note that the folding leg must be shorter than the distance from the table to the floor, so that it will fold and fit within that space. Position the leg hinge about 6 inches below the rear edge of the table to shorten the folded leg. It is necessary for the end of the table to reach as far down as possible so there is room for the folded leg when the table is in its down position.

## Featherboards

These handy hold-down devices do what your hands do in places where it is unsafe or inconvenient for your hands to be. Make a featherboard by taking a piece of any kind of wood.at about $3/4"\times4"\times30"$, and cutting a 45° angle on one end. Then make kerfs about 4" long in that end on the band saw or table saw. Make the individual feathers on the board about $1/8"$ thick or so. Clamp the featherboards in place on your machine table or fence so that when the work is passed by them the feathers deflect about $1/16"$, or just enough to hold the work in place.

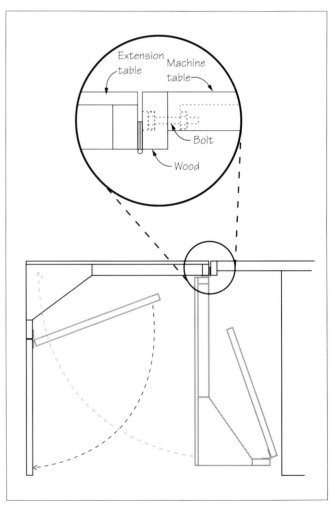

*Using a hinge, attach the extraction table to the machine table.*

*Featherboards on a table saw.*

*Featherboards on a router table.*

*One style of push stick.*

*A second style of push stick.*

## Push Sticks

It's easy to be safe at the table saw by taking simple precautions. When you cut pieces that are less than 3" wide, use push sticks to keep your fingers clear of the blade. Here are two designs for push sticks. Whichever one you use is a matter of personal preference. Make either type out of scrap solid stock or plywood. It's OK to let the blade cut the push stick itself during the cut, so long as there is still enough of the push stick to move the piece through. After the push stick has been cut a few times, it's time to toss it and make some more.

## Resaw Fence

Resaw means cutting a board along its edge to yield two boards of lesser thickness. This is usually done on a band saw, but you can also do it on a table saw. A table saw blade removes a thicker kerf than a band saw however, which means you get less wood and more chips, and a table saw can only resaw boards of

width twice the height of the blade above the table. One alternative for boards wider than twice this height is to make table saw cuts on the edge of a board as far as the saw will cut, then cut the rest on the band saw.

When you do resaw on the band saw, you need a fence to hold the stock at a set distance from the blade. There are two approaches to this. The first is a point-location fence, which contacts the work only along a point immediately adjacent to the blade. The other is a long fence, which supports the work along a broad flat face during the cut.

The point-location fence has two advantages. First, if the blade begins to wander one way or the other during the cut, you can tilt the work to compensate and straighten the cut. Secondly, if you want to resaw stock that is not flat, this fence lets you follow a bowed face.

A long fence is harder to use because you must align the direction of cut parallel with the fence. You

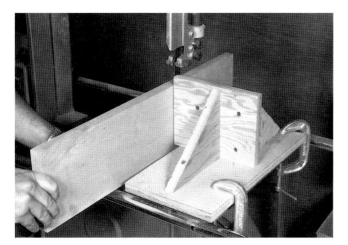

Point location resaw fence.

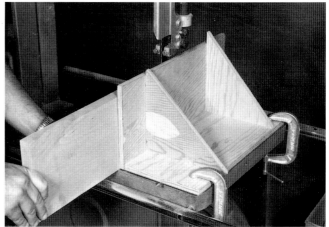

Long fence for resaw.

Setup to bore for dowels on the drill press.

Space adjacent dowels with a spacer at the end stop.

can't alter the direction of the work into the blade once you start. But the chief advantage of a long fence is that, when adjusted properly, it makes a straight and uniform cut.

Use a wide blade for resawing, and tighten it for minimum deflection. Use a blade with only two or three teeth per inch so that there is plenty of chip clearance during the long cut. Don't force the work into the blade, let it cut at the rate that it wants to. Make practice cuts with scrap stock first to test the variables. Use a push stick at the end of the cut so your fingers are clear of the blade.

### Drill Press Edge Boring for Fence

The drill press is the best place to bore holes for dowels in the edge of stock when the parts are small enough to easily fit on the machine. The fences you can clamp to the drill press table make the hole locations very accurate, and the rigidity of the machine itself guarantees that holes will be consistently perpendicular to the face into which they are bored.

Place a long board onto the drill press table. This

will support the other end of pieces as they are bored. This base board must be perpendicular to the line of boring. Check this by putting a square against it and the bit in the chuck. Next clamp a vertical fence on top of the base board and drill press table. Use a thick piece of scrap for stability. Check to be sure that the face of the fence is parallel to the bit.

Clamp an end stop onto the base board to establish the distance from the holes to the end of your stock. Rather than moving the end stop to bore each of adjacent holes, use a spacer between the end stop and the part to bore the second hole.

### Making Doweling Jigs

A doweling jig functions rather simply—it aligns your drill bit in a certain location while you bore the hole with your hand drill. Each manufactured doweling jig has a different mechanism for doing that, and each mechanism will locate holes in certain places and not in others. Few manufactured jigs will locate a hole in the middle of a 10"-wide board; all will locate a hole on a board's edge.

When you want to locate holes where manufactured jigs can't, and where it's impossible or inconvenient with a drill press, make your own jig. Shop-made doweling jigs are not as easy to use as manufactured jigs, but will align holes anywhere that you can clamp down the jig and get a drill in location.

There are two aspects to making an accurate jig. The first is boring an accurate guide hole. Use dense hardwood stock like oak or walnut. The guide hole you bore in it must be perpendicular to the face of the guide block. The only way to do this accurately is with a drill press or a doweling jig, the former being more accurate. Use the same bit to bore the guide that you intend to use for the holes to be bored with the guide. Check the hole for accuracy by putting a dowel part way into it and then putting a square up to the dowel.

The second aspect is attaching a fence or plate onto

the block so you can hold it where you want. The first photo shows a block located in the middle of a wide board. The block is attached to a piece of plywood, and the plywood has a fence on it that rides against the edge of the board. This fence determines the distance of the hole from the board's edge. Where the hole is located is determined by carefully measuring and clamping the jig down in the right spot.

The second photo shows a jig used to locate holes on the end of a 2"-wide part. Manufactured doweling jigs do this easily, but a drill press won't, so if all you have is a drill press, do your end boring like this, and your edge boring on the drill press. With this jig the block is attached to a piece of plywood, and the jig and part are clamped together in a vise. To guarantee that the end of the part is perpendicular to the guide hole, scribe a line on the plywood parallel to the guide hole. Align the edge of the part against this line.

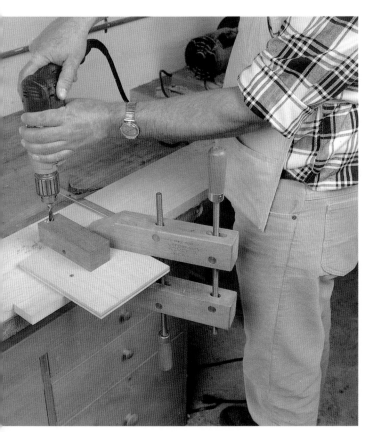

*Boring a hole in the middle of a wide board with a shop-made dowel jig.*

*End boring with a shop-made dowel jig.*

# 16 BUYING JIGS AND FIXTURES

There is a wide variety of ready-made jigs and fixtures available through mail order. This chapter discusses some of those that I think have the broadest use for home enthusiasts. There is some overlap between these jigs and those described in previous chapters, but notice that each jig, be it one you make or one you buy, has different capabilities. To decide which you want to make or buy, look closely at the capabilities of each and decide which one you need to do the job.

## Tenoning and Mortising Tools

The four tools shown on these two pages can all be used to make mortise and tenon joints with a router or table saw, or both. The first two shown in the photos at right are tenoning attachments that run in a guide channel in either a table saw or router table. Probably the best advantage that these tools have over shop-made tenoning jigs is the machined metal, which holds its alignment very well.

Unfortunately, one disadvantage of both these tools is that they don't employ a screw mechanism for adjusting the distance of the work from the cutter. That doesn't mean they can't be used accurately, but it does mean that you must be very careful when making adjustments. To make adjustments, loosen the handle on the jig base and move the 90° bracket by hand. The best way to move something in very small increments is to loosen the handle until it just barely grips, then tap the tool with a soft hammer or chunk of wood, looking carefully to see how far it moves. By trial and error you will be able to fit tenons snugly into mortises.

The first jig is sold by Leichtung and is made out of aluminum. The face of the 90° bracket has many holes for support pins (provided) and angle lines to help you line up parts for cuts away from 90°. It comes with two clamps like those shown.

The second jig is made by Bryco and comes with a small toggle clamp for securing the work. This tool is made of steel and aluminum, and is a bit heavier than the Leichtung model.

Since guide channels on different table saws vary in width, each of these manufacturers had to make its

Photo 1—Leichtung Universal Tenoning Tool.

Photo 2—Bryco Tenoning attachment.

tool adjustable in some way to fit different channels. The Leichtung model does so with a screw-mounted double bar that can be expanded or contracted to fit different channels. The Bryco model has a solid steel bar that fits the channel, and the instructions suggest that you file or grind it to fit if it's too large. It fit my saw fine with no alterations necessary.

## Router Tenoning Jigs

Photo 3 shows the Porter Cable Mor-ten jig, which makes the joint in the picture plus several variations. You get the plate steel template and router bit shown, as well as a guide bracket that the template sits on. The steel jig is very sturdy and will hold up a long time.

The jig makes basically one joint of a fixed depth and width, which will limit its application. But, the joint is of an average size that can be used in many furniture applications, and once set up you can make joints with it very quickly.

Note that to make the mortise with this jig you must plunge the bit within the oval hole in the surface of the template. Once you have plunged it all the way in, you rub the follower bearing on the bit around the oval to complete the cut. The manufacturer's instructions suggest that you make this plunge cut with a fixed base, rather than with a plunge router. This is dangerous at best, because you or the bit could cause the router to twitch, sending the bit into the steel template. I suggest that you use this jig with a plunge router only for safety.

Photo 4 shows the Rig-A-Mortise router base attachment, which causes your router to be centered over the work by rubbing the two plastic dowels on opposing faces of the piece. This is a simple, ingenious idea that works very well. The router is a bit unstable on the edge of a thin board as in the photo, but the instructions give designs for several simple jigs that place wood on either side of your work to stabilize the cut and still make use of the centering effect.

This jig won't cut tenons, but the instructions give you a simple design for a tenoning setup for your router. This jig won't make joints quite as fast as the Porter Cable, but it gives you more range of joint sizes and configurations.

## Dovetail Jigs

Before you buy any dovetail jig, ask yourself seriously if you intend to use it very much. The expense and effort aren't really justified unless you use it often. If you just need a few joints, do them by hand, or use the shop-made dovetailing jig shown in chapter

*Photo 3—Porter Cable Mor-Ten jig.*

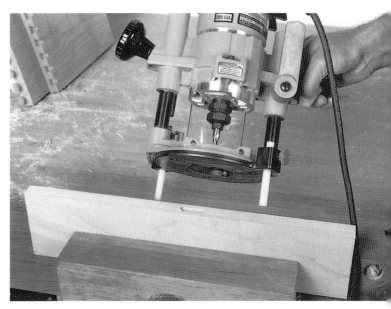
*Photo 4—Rig-A-Mortise router attachment.*

eleven. If you want to make a lot of dovetails, such as on all the drawers for the workbench in this book, then consider a jig. Dovetail jigs take a while to set up and some are costly, but once they are set up, you can make a lot of tight-fitting joints in very little time.

There is a wide range of jigs available, as you'll see. Generally, the more expensive jigs are better made and offer wider capabilities. If you are fascinated by intricate devices, you'll have a field day with some of the more complicated dovetail jigs. On the other hand, if you just want a simple device for making half-blind dovetails, there are several less expensive devices that are simpler to use.

All dovetail jigs work on a similar principle,

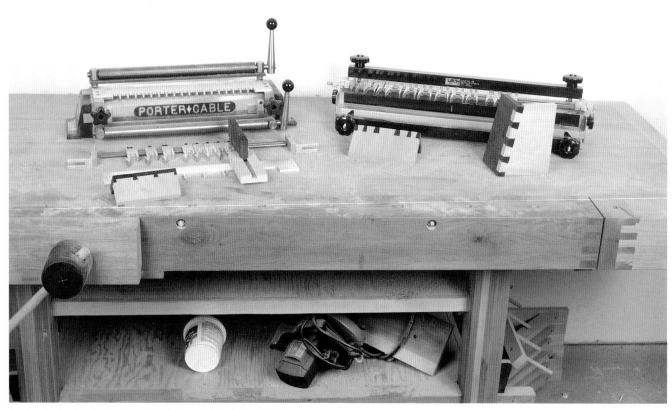

*Photo 1—Porter Cable Omnijig (left) and Leigh jig (right).*

though each accomplishes this in a different way. All jigs provide templates that you place onto the wood and that guide a router bit along the edge of the wood to cut the dovetails and pins. Dovetails (the part that looks like the tail of a dove) are always cut with a dovetail bit, which is a straight flute bit with the flutes set at an angle. The pins (the parts that fit between the dovetails) are cut either with a straight flute bit with parallel sides (through dovetails), or with the same dovetail bit that cut the dovetails themselves (half-blind dovetails).

Either way, the spacing between the dovetails depends entirely on the configuration of the templates. This has been the curse of dovetail templates, because perfectly spaced dovetails look too "machine made" for the tastes of hand tool woodworkers. Also, if you cannot vary the space between dovetails, you must design the heights of drawers or other part dimensions in increments equal to the distance between dovetails on your template; otherwise, the part ends with a half or quarter dovetail which looks bad (though doesn't affect strength).

Some jigs allow you to vary the space between dovetails with adjustable templates, or with fixed-space templates. This added feature has its cost both monetarily and in terms of complexity. The adjustable template jigs are the most expensive, and it takes longer to learn how to use them. But they are not as incomprehensible as legal fine print, and once you figure out the process you can set the jigs up quickly.

The photo above shows two of the more expensive, and certainly the most versatile, of jigs available. They are the Porter Cable Omnijig, and the Leigh jig. The manufacturers of both these jigs have as their goal to make versatile dovetailing devices, given the limitations of a router and jigs. Both have done an excellent job at this.

The Leigh jig uses a unique template setup with a series of finger guides mounted on parallel bars. Each of the fingers has a set screw that locks it in place, and thus the fingers can slide back and forth on the parallel bars to any location. This flexibility gives the jig infinite spacing of all dovetails in any configuration. The jig is made from a large aluminum extrusion with various clamping bars and other attachments for fixing the wood to the jig. Two models are available, a 12" and 24". The jig comes with a thorough instruction book. An informative video is

**Photo 2—Keller dovetail templates (left) and Dovemaster
templates (right).**

also available.

First you configure the fingers according to your desires, then follow the instructions for flipping the finger assembly this way or that depending on the type of joint you want to make. The jig can be used to make through, half-blind, sliding, and end-to-end dovetails. In addition, the instructions tell how to make angled joints (test piece on right in photo), "cogged" dovetails (where the pin thicknesses vary), and spline joints. A supplementary template is available for cutting mortise and tenon joints for joining shelves to carcass sides.

The Porter Cable Omnijig uses different templates for each joint it cuts. When you wish to cut a different type of joint, you replace the template on top of the jig and proceed with specific instructions for that template. Three of the templates are shown in the photo. The jig is made from a large, heavy aluminum casting, and it's securing levers with cam-action holding bars are of heavy steel, which is extremely rugged. It comes in both 16" and 24" models. Templates are available for cutting two sizes of half-blind dovetails, adjustably spaced through dovetails, 2"-spaced half-blind dovetails, tapered sliding dovetails, and a box joint, or finger joint. A thorough book of instructions explains procedures, and an explanatory video is available.

The template in photo 1 on the bench closest to the Omnijig has adjustable fingers that can be spaced for variably spaced through dovetails. The template on the bench farthest from the jig is for making half-blind dovetails that are spaced 2" apart, as in the test

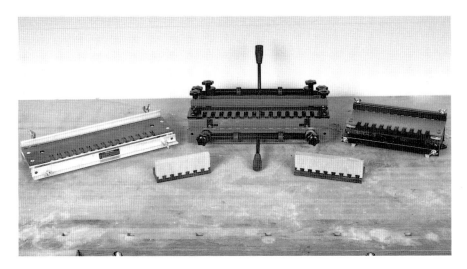

Photo 3—Porter Cable dovetail jig (left), AMT jig (center) and Vermont American jig (right).

Photo 4—Wolfcraft dovetailer with special router base (left) and Leichtung Dovetail and Mortise/Tenon jig (right).

piece on the left in the photo. The template on the jig makes half-blind dovetails similar to those shown in the photos.

### Keller and Dovemaster Templates

The jigs in photo 2 (page 49) consist only of templates that you mount onto fences, and then clamp to your workpieces. The advantage here is simplicity—there are far fewer adjustments to make, and you can cut out joints very quickly. Also, you can cut joints of unlimited length by simply sliding the jig along the end of the work. The disadvantage is that they cut fewer types of joints. What they do best is cut through dovetails spaced at the template spacings. They will not cut half-blind dovetails. They can be used to cut variably spaced through joints, but this requires that you align them very carefully. These jigs are an excellent choice for cutting dovetails to join carcasses.

The Keller templates are made of ½" plate aluminum that is precisely machined. Models available are 16", 24" and 36". Good quality router bits come

with the templates. These bits have follower bearings that prevent wear on the templates. The Keller templates will outlive you if you take care of them.

The Dovemaster templates are made of plastic, and come in two sizes. The separate templates cut joints with different spacings, giving you a choice. Bits do not come with the templates, and the jigs use a template guide that does come with the jig to guide the router through the cut.

### Half-Blind Jigs

These three jigs (photo 3) all do one thing only—cut half-blind dovetails. They can do so within a rabbet as shown in the test piece on the right in the photo, or flush against the part edge as shown (left).

The Porter Cable jig (left) is made of steel with a plastic template. Wing nuts hold the work on the jig, and its maximum width of cut is 12".

The AMT jig (center) is also made of steel with a plastic template. It is the largest and heaviest of the three, and has lever and cam clamps for securing the work to the template. Maximum width of cut is 12".

The Vermont American jig is made entirely of plastic. It uses wing nuts to hold the work down, and takes work 8" wide.

A critical adjustment on this type of jig is the projection of the template beyond the front of the jig. The projection determines the depth of the pin cut. The Porter Cable handles this precisely with a set screw and Allen wrench. The AMT is set by hand by sliding parts secured with knobs; and the Vermont American jig uses lever actuated plastic cams, which is simple but effective.

## Wolfcraft and Leichtung

The Wolfcraft dovetailing fixture (photo 4, page 50) consists of a cast aluminum grid and a special router base, which locks into sliding grooves in the grid. Various adjustments and settings allow it to accomplish what the three previous jigs do—half-blind

dovetails. Because of its design it is not limited to specific widths of stock. With a special indexing peg (included) it can be slid along the edge of stock for making very wide joints.

The Leichtung dovetail/mortise and tenon fixture in photo 4 is a fairly complicated collection of various guides and templates which can be used to cut everything from simple finger joints to mortise and tenon joints and even half-blind dovetails of any width. The mortise and tenon template is similar in design to the Porter Cable Mor-Ten template, using a plunge cut within an oval hole for the mortise. Again, I recommend that you use only a plunge router for this operation. This fixture is fairly complicated, but that's because it's designed to do a lot in one package.

## Doweling Jigs

Before buying a doweling jig, understand what kind

| | Record | Stanley | Dowl-it | Dowel Craft | Leichtung | Arco |
|---|---|---|---|---|---|---|
| Guide sizes supplied | 6, 8, 9mm 1/4", 3/8" | 3/16, 1/4, 5/16 3/8, 7/16, 1/2" | 1/4, 5/16 3/8, 7/16, 1/2" | 1/4, 5/16 3/8, 1/2" | 1/4, 5/16 3/8, 1/2" | 1/4, 5/16 3/8" |
| | X | X | X | X | no | X |
| | X | X to 2 7/8" thick stock | limited use | X to 2 3/4" thick stock | no | to 2 1/4" thick stock |
| | X | X | X | X | no | X |
| | X | no | no | no | no | no |
| | X | X | X | X | X | X |
| | X | no | no | no | no | X |

*Use this chart to compare the variety of doweling jigs available.*

*Photo 1—Record dowel jig (left), Dowl-It jig (center) and Stanley jig (right).*

of joints each jig will handle, and what kind it won't. Some excel at making certain kinds of joints, yet are completely incapable of producing others. This chart shows the types of joints most commonly used with dowels, and which jigs will make them and which ones won't. There are other jigs available besides those shown here, and when you consider another jig, look closely to see what it will do.

The photo above shows the Record, Dowl-It and Stanley jigs. The Record is by far the most versatile of all doweling jigs—capable of making every joint I can

think of that you might put a dowel into. To make some of these joints however, you will need longer parallel bars, which can be ordered from the manufacturer. The jig is shown in the photo aligning holes for a miter joint along the edge of a board.

While the Record jig is capable of any type of joint, that doesn't mean its the easiest to use. The big advantage to the Dowl-It jig is that it is very quick and easy to use for centering holes on the edge or end of stock. The threaded spindle pulls or pushes the two outside plates simultaneously, keeping the middle

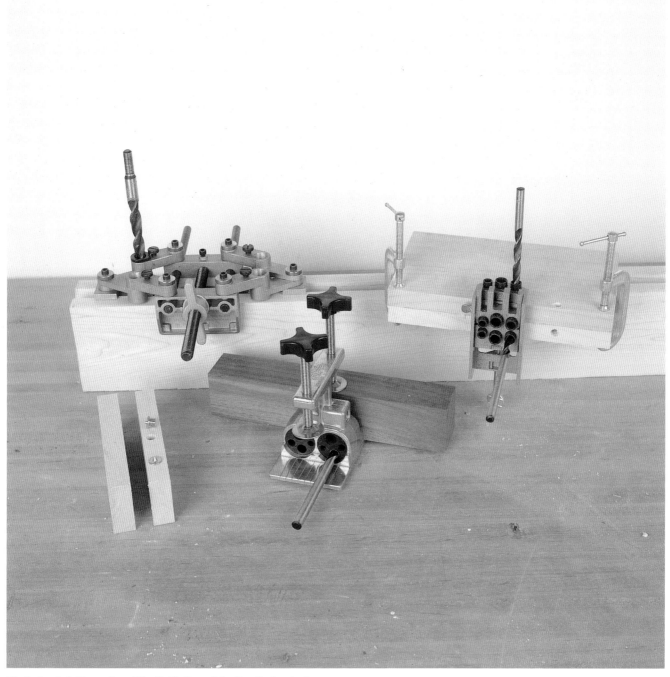

*Photo 2—Leichtung dowel jig (left), Dowel Crafter jig (center) and Arco jig (left).*

guide block centered between them at all times. Off-center holes are possible, but less convenient because you must place shims of the correct thickness between the work and one of the plates. This becomes problematic because the plates only move so far apart.

The Stanley jig is good at locating off-center holes. It has a sliding guide block that allows you to place the drill guide anywhere along the surface that the jig is clamped to. This jig sets the hole at a given distance from one edge of your stock, rather than centering it between two faces, like the Dowl-It. The Stanley jig,

therefore, has the advantage of letting you join boards of different thickness with one face—the reference face—flush.

The photo above shows the Leichtung, Dowl Crafter and Arco jigs. The Leichtung jig is similar to the Dowl-It because it centers the hole over the edge of stock, but it differs because it sets up on two boards at once for a total of four holes per setup. This makes it very fast for edge joining boards, but of little use for other jobs.

The Dowel Crafter's unique design makes it fast to

*Photo 1—Mortising attachments like this are available for most models of drill presses.*

set up and use. Like the Stanley jig, it references off one face rather than uses a centering action, so it's especially useful for drilling offset holes. It will bore two holes at one setup. Boring can be done from either side of the jig, and indeed each side of your joint should be done with opposing sides of the jig to maintain alignment of the holes. Extra long bits (available from the manufacturer) are required to reach over the holding plates on either side of the jig.

The Arco jig is the only one, besides the Record, that will locate holes for a shelf on the end or in the middle of a board. This is its chief advantage, though it is capable of various edge-boring operations like most of the others. How the jig aligns holes is a bit hard to visualize at first, but the instructions walk you through it, and once you see how it works it is easy to use.

## Miscellaneous Tools

A mortising chisel attached to your drill press allows the machine to do the seemingly impossible—bore square holes (photo 1). It does so by surrounding a circular drill bit with a square chisel that punches corners around the hole as the bit clears out the waste in the center. This allows you to quickly make mortises that don't need to have their ends squared up by hand, as is necessary when you make mortises with a router.

But, alas and alack, the mortising chisel doesn't always work as well as it sounds. The hardness of the wood is a critical factor. You won't have much trouble in pine, but oak and other hardwoods are tough for a mortising chisel to cut through. Sometimes the chisel gets stuck in the bottom of the hole, and won't easily pull out. You can put paraffin on the chisel to ease its entry and exit, but wax can ruin the glue bond on a piece of wood.

Be certain that you get a mortising attachment that will fit your drill press. The bracket that holds the chisel attaches to the quill above your chuck, and the internal diameter of the bracket must match the quill. Your drill press manufacturer should be able to supply you with the right attachment. Be sure to indicate the model number and quill diameter.

Tapered drill bits with countersinks are real time-savers when you need to install screws (photo 2, page 55). The tapered bit makes a hole that roughly approximates the shape of the screws. Properly used, this guarantees that the screw is gripping wood well at the threads, rather than splitting the wood like a nail or spinning in a hole that's too big.

My set of bits came in a plastic envelope that has screw sizes printed on it for each size bit, but I rarely follow these numbers. The size you use should vary with the hardness of the wood you are putting screws into. For a #8 screw in pine, I'll use the #6 bit, but for the same screw in oak I might use the #9 bit so the screw just drops in until the last 3/8" or so. Pine crushes so much that you need more wood there to grip. Oak doesn't, and will quickly grip a screw tight enough to shear it off if the hole is too small. Do tests in scrap to find the right size bit and the best location for the countersink from the end of the bit, given your screw size and length.

A speedy combination for installing screws is to use a tapered bit with countersink on one drill, and a Phillips screw tip in a variable-speed drill driver. If you have a lot of screws to install, this combination allows you to quickly punch holes and ease the screws in with a gentle touch on the trigger.

The countersinks have an added plus. The hole they make is just the right size to hold a wooden plug to hide the hole. Plug cutters are simple tools that you put into the drill press and cut plugs out of scrap.

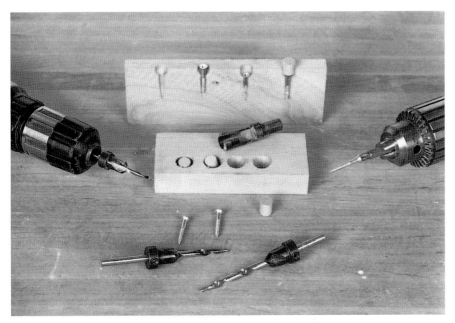

*Photo 2—Tapered drill bits with countersinks are the best way to install screws.*

*Photo 3—Wedge-type hold-down sold by Woodcraft (left) and screw type sold by Record (right).*

Both plug cutters and tapered drill bits are readily available in hardware stores and through any wood-oriented mail order catalog.

Hold-downs for your bench top are very handy for clamping down pieces in the middle of the bench where you can't get any other clamps. This photo shows two types. On the left is an old-style hold-down that has been in use for centuries. You simply hit it into a hole in the top, and the wedging action of the bar against the sides of the hole is enough to cause it to, well, hold down. To loosen it, you hit it on the side with your hammer.

The second screw-type hold-down is a bit more mechanically secure, and will apply more pressure than the wedge. Its vertical bar enters a special fitting installed in the bench top, which has ridges that match the ridges in the bar. When the bar is at an angle in the fitting, the ridges engage, locking the two together. The screw applies a surprising amount of pressure given that its arm and pressure foot are a good distance away. Always use blocks on top of your work so the hold-downs don't mar the surface.

# PART 2

# PROJECTS

When I first took up woodworking and began to collect tools, I stored them in my garage in a few card board boxes stacked in the corner. Gradually my collection grew, and the containers for them grew in number and variety, including an old wooden army ammo box, plastic five-gallon buckets, a couple of old drawers, and more cardboard boxes. These stayed stacked neatly in the corner until I needed to find something, whereupon I would begin to dig through the containers, shuffling them around behind and alongside me until I found what I wanted.

One day I went out to the garage to find a carpet awl I had procured in a yard sale some time back and which I knew was in the stack somewhere. Unfortunately it wasn't in one of the first few boxes or buckets I looked in, so pretty soon I was surrounded by precariously perched piles of tool-laden containers set atop one another as I continued to dig through the stack. When I pulled one of the last boxes toward me, what did I see behind it but the neighbor's cat with a dead rat in its mouth. The cat must have thought that I was after his prey, because he growled and began taking swipes at me. I jerked back suddenly, but hit my boxes and lost my balance, falling with arms and legs flailing about. I must have accidentally kicked the cat in my desperate attempt to regain balance, or he leapt up in the air out of fear at my reaction to his attack, either way I saw him and the rat flying through the air as the tools, boxes and myself came crashing to the floor. The cat scurried out the door terrified, but without his rat. I'm not going to tell you where that rodent ended up.

Anyway, it was at that moment, as I lay buried in tools, broken drawers and cardboard, that I resolved to build myself a set of shop cabinets. Somehow I found solace in the vision of several chests of drawers, and maybe a toolbox too. How nice they would look against the wall, neatly organized with any tool I wanted just a drawer pull away. Of course they couldn't prevent the neighbor's cat from scaring the daylights out of me again, but they would keep the results of another such encounter from being a disaster. So after cleaning up the mess, I immediately went to the drawing board to come up with a design.

The workbench on cabinet of drawers in chapter nineteen is what I came up with. This workbench-cabinet combination is a good choice for a bench if you have a construction from building these, and it will help you with future furniture projects. The bulk of work here entails joinery for numerous frames which make a carcass or box. Note that the next project, the grinder cabinet, uses the same joinery techniques and can be built simultaneously with this project.

A workbench of this type presents one problem: When you have a large piece of work in the vise, it often blocks the drawers from opening. For that reason it is nice, if you have the space, to keep your bench and storage separate. In this case the traditional workbench design presented in chapter seventeen is favorable. If you build this bench, you might also want to build either or both of the wall-mounted cabinets (chapters twenty-three and twenty-four) for more storage.

Traditional bench designs like this were meant to provide a work surface that was as stable as a rock. When woodworking was done entirely by hand, a heavy, rigid bench was essential because joiners had to hold work still as they applied tools to it. While this is less necessary for a woodworker who plans to primarily use machine techniques, it's still desirable. There's nothing more irritating than a wobbly bench, no matter what you're doing! The traditional tail-vise in conjunction with bench dogs provides a convenient means of clamping down work for hand planing, routing and belt sanding.

If you are a beginner, I suggest that you first read chapter thirty-nine, which gives advice about how to approach projects. Then start with a few simpler projects like the table top router table and the large toolbox, before taking on a large project like one of the benches. And if you do stack your tools in the corner in boxes and buckets, remember to leave a little catnip *outside* the shop door!

# 17 TRADITIONAL WORKBENCH

**P**urchasing thick timbers for a project like this can be very expensive. Such timbers are often several times more costly per board foot than 1× lumber. Laminate 1× lumber together to make timber thickness, and the top is therefore much cheaper. Additionally, you can incorporate most of the mortise and tenon joints into the laminations themselves, saving yourself much labor and producing excellent joinery.

This is the best place to use up your knotted, ugly and twisted stock. Even if a piece has a knot or defect large enough that it would break if you stressed it at all, it will be fine inside a lamination, so long as adjoining areas on adjacent boards are good. There are knots the size of your fist inside my laminations. You can't see them because they are located between

*Build this sturdy bench by gluing together layers of thin stock to get thick, heavy timbers.*

layers, and the whole laminated timber is plenty strong because of its large size. Likewise, twisted pieces straighten out when clamped up as all the parts are pulled together.

To create accurate joinery within the laminations, and to ensure that the edges of the laminations will line up fairly close, it's important to prepare the stock carefully. Look ahead and you'll see how the layers are held in alignment with dowels placed in alignment holes. These holes must be located accurately on all pieces so that they will line up well, and you can't place the holes well unless your stock is consistent. Therefore, ripping to width and cutting to length must be done accurately.

Get out the parts as shown on the cutting list. Use knots and defects as mentioned before, but try to place them away from joinery areas, and also try to have enough clear pieces to use on the outer laminations so that they will look nice. Use your straight-edge jig (chapter five) to straighten one edge on all your pieces. This is very important, and if you haven't built this jig and don't have a jointer, now is the time to build it.

Once you have a straight edge on all parts, rip them to width on your table saw, and cut them off square at the radial arm, or with the table saw cutoff box shown in chapter eight. Use the end stop shown in that chapter to ensure that pieces of the same length are indeed the same length.

There are four pieces that get cut off at 10°, rather than square. These are the center end laminations for the stretcher wedge mortises, which must be angled to accept the wedges that hold the stretchers to the

*Secure the bench top to the top rails with a lag screw at the front and a sliding keeper at the rear. The sliding keeper allows the bench top to move with moisture variations.*

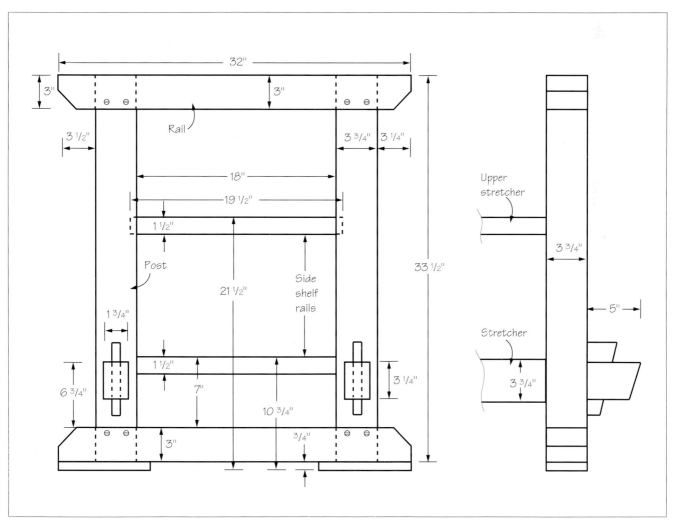

*The posts and rails for the bench support assemblies are joined with mortises and tenons incorporated into the laminated layers.*

posts. Make these angled cuts with your miter gauge at the table saw.

Cut notches in the middle layers of the post laminations for the small shelf rails that run between the posts. Use your miter gauge at the table saw as shown in photo 1 to cut kerfs within the area of the notch. Use the rip fence as a guide to locate the outer two cuts. Make these ¾" deep, and clean out the waste with a chisel.

Set up at the drill press to bore alignment holes in the laminations, as shown in photo 2. You could use a doweling jig to bore these holes (but only certain doweling jigs will work across these larger widths), or make your own doweling jig as in chapter fifteen. A drill press is the easiest way to position the holes accurately. Bore two holes in each piece to guarantee that it will be aligned during the glue up. You might think that you can align the parts during glue up without dowels, by tapping them back and forth as you tighten the clamps. You can also build a ladder to the moon if you have enough lumber.

Seriously, glue is slippery and as the clamps are tightened, parts will slip and slide, making alignment difficult at best. For the major mortise and tenon joints on the posts and rails to be tight, the parts must be very close, and dowels are your best insurance. Photo 3 shows how the mortise laminations for the rails and stretchers will appear after boring. The posts are similar, but since they have tenons rather than mortises they simply have one longer piece, the center lamination, and its ends become the tenons (see photo 7, page 62). Use a ¹⁷⁄₆₄" bit to bore the holes, and use ¼" dowels. The slightly oversize hole will not resist the dowels, and still align the parts well.

Use brown glue for the glue up. Properly called plastic resin urea formaldehyde glue, brown glue has two major advantages over yellow glue (aliphatic polyvinyl acetate). First, it has a long open time, which means it doesn't begin to grip right away so you have lots of time to deal with your parts. Secondly, it is highly water resistant, so if your bench is exposed to water, the laminations won't come apart. Use the glue in a well-ventilated area because formaldehyde is poisonous.

You'll need about 15 lbs. of glue for the whole bench, including the top. Roll the glue on with 3"-wide paint rollers as shown in photo 4 (page 61). Don't try to clean the roller when you are done, just toss it. Apply a thick layer of glue to all adjoining surfaces as you put the layers together. The bare wood will absorb a lot of the glue so be sure to apply plenty.

Photo 1—Cut mortises in the center post laminations for the smaller shelf support rails. Set up on the table saw with a miter gauge, and use the rip fence to establish the distance of the cuts from the end.

Photo 2—Align the laminations to each other with dowels in carefully located holes. Set up on the drill press to accurately place the holes.

Photo 3—Make mortises in the rails and stretchers by leaving voids in the center laminations. Note that each piece must have at least two dowels to ensure that it stays properly located.

Do the four rails together, then the four posts, and lastly the two stretchers. But don't apply glue to one of these three groups until you've clamped up the previous! Place one layer of wax paper between each of the rails, posts or stretchers to keep them from getting glued together, and clamp up as in photo 5. Lift the clamps ½" off the wood so you can clean the glue underneath. Use very hot water to clean off as much glue as possible. It's easier to clean it now— later you have to sand it off. Clean out the mortises by placing a rag inside each mortise and moving it up and down as shown.

Brown glue dries overnight in warm weather, and takes longer in cold weather. When you run out of clamps, belt sand the parts with a 30-grit belt to remove remaining glue and level out the layers, which won't be perfectly aligned. Then belt sand again with 80-grit and then 120 if you like.

Set up a ¾"-wide dado in your table saw and raise it to ⁵⁄₁₆" above the table. Use this to cut around all four sides on the ends of the stretchers to a distance of 8¾" from their ends. This effectively makes the ends of these parts into tenons that will fit through mortises in the posts. Use a sharp chisel to clean up the ugly marks left by the dado.

The only mortises you must chop by hand are in the posts for the stretchers. Note the exact size of the stretcher tenons, and mark out the posts at this size. Bore holes within your marks to clear out most of the waste in the mortises, then use chisels to complete them as shown in photo 6 (page 61). Gradually widen the mortises until the stretchers slide in neatly. The completed joints for the rails, posts and stretchers should appear as in photo 7 (page 61). Note that you must also cut shallow mortises for the lighter shelf stretchers that go above the main stretchers.

Cut angles on the ends of the rails at the table saw with the miter gauge and your blade set at 45°. Screw feet pads onto the bottom of the lower rails using brass screws, which won't rust. Test the fit of the post tenons into the rail mortises and trim the tenons if necessary. Pull the rail and post assemblies together with clamps, and don't use any glue. Glue isn't necessary because the joints are so large that they can be held together with screws. Besides, glue probably wouldn't adhere because the mortise walls already have dried glue from the lamination. Don't forget to put in the short shelf rails between the posts before you put the rails on the posts.

Bore holes for and install two 3" brass screws in each of the post-rail joints as shown in the drawing. These will only guarantee that the tenons won't come out of the mortises should the joints loosen from the

**Photo 4—Glue together the laminations using a 3"-wide paint roller. Use a lot of glue, and have hot water and rags close by to deal with the mess.**

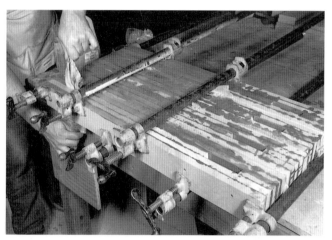

**Photo 5—Gang clamp the laminations together, then use very hot water to remove as much glue as possible from the outside of the pieces and within the mortises.**

# MATERIALS LIST

| Part | Dimension |
| --- | --- |
| All stock ¾" thick unless otherwise noted. | |
| A  Posts (16) | 3¾" × 27½" |
| B  Posts (4) | 3¾" × 33½" |
| C  Rails (16) | 3" × 32" |
| D  Rails (4) | 3" × 18" |
| E  Rails (8) | 3" × 3¼" |
| F  Rail feet (4) | 3¾" × 10" |
| G  Lower stretchers (4) | 3" × 60" |
| H  Lower stretchers (2) | 3" × 50" |
| I  Upper stretchers (2) | 1½" × 44" |
| J  Side shelf rails (4) | 1½" × 19½" |
| K  Top laminations (48) | 1½" × 84" |

Photo 6—Cut mortises in the posts for the lower stretchers. Mark out the mortises, bore holes within the marks, then clean out the waste with chisel and hammer.

Photo 7—Trim the walls of the stretcher mortises until the stretcher tenons slide in easily for rapid assembly and disassembly. The post tenons into the rail mortises can be a tighter fit, since they will go in only once.

Photo 8—Set up the laminations for the bench top with dowels to orient each layer. Also bore holes in each layer for a threaded rod that will hold together the separate slabs of the top.

gradual effects of moisture variation. But the strength of the joints comes from the mechanical fit of the tenons in the mortises, which you guaranteed by the careful alignment of the laminated joint components.

Set the stretchers in the post mortises, and make wedges to tighten them. Make these wedges on the table saw with the taper jig from chapter three. Attach shelf support cleats around the inside perimeters of the upper shelf stretchers and main stretchers. Cut out plywood shelves to fit within, and notch the corners of the shelves to fit around the posts. Fix the shelves down with a few screws.

Use the same dowel alignment procedure to laminate together three plates for the bench top. But also bore four sets of $9/16$" holes in the layers for threaded rod to run through. This rod will hold all three plates together. Your bench top layers will appear as in photo 8 prior to gluing up. Again, you can use stock with knots and other defects, but turn those defects toward the underside, and try to get one clean edge on each layer. Straightening the edges of the layers is, as before, very important.

Glue up each of the plates as in photo 9 (page 63). There is a serious danger when gluing up a long lamination like this that it will not be flat. The clamping pressure tends to twist it, like an Oriental fan opening. To prevent this, place winding sticks on either end of the glue up to check the alignment. These are simply straight boards that show you whether both ends of the lamination are parallel. Place the sticks perpendicular to the laminations. Align your sight along the tops of the two winding

sticks, and you will quickly see if the two tops are parallel. If they are not, the lamination is "unwinding" and you need to loosen the clamps, tweak the layers, and clamp up again. You won't be able to get it perfect, but you need to get it fairly close. The router planing jig will flatten minor twisting, but it won't make a silk purse out of a sow's ear.

Flatten the plates with a router planing setup as in photo 10 (page 63) after the glue is dry. Use a 1"-wide straight flute carbide bit to plane the surface. How flat the resulting surface will be depends on how carefully you set up the guides that the router travels along during the cut. Check and double check your setup before you cut.

The setup consists of two major components. The first is the base to which the router is attached. This is simply two guide bars with a piece of plywood between them to which the router base is screwed. These two bars must be parallel and straight.

The second component is the combination of long guide bars and clamps that you attach to the laminated plate. There are two things to watch for here. First, the two bars must be parallel, and you can check that with winding sticks placed perpendicular across the bars as described above. Secondly, you must locate the top of the plate itself at a uniform distance from the top edges of the two guide bars. It can't be closer to the guide bars on one end than it is on the other. Since the plate isn't flat you can't get it at a perfectly uniform distance everywhere and still keep the bars parallel, but you must get the distances as close as possible to each other given the amount of

Photo 9—*When you glue and clamp the slabs, you must ensure that they stay reasonably flat. The layers can "wind" like an Oriental fan, producing an interesting sculpture that is useless as a bench top.*

Photo 10—*Flatten each slab with this router planing setup. The two long guide rails that the router jig rides on must be parallel to each other. The slab surface must be a uniform distance from the long guide rails at all points, or close to it.*

out-of-flat you are dealing with.

Set the router depth to cut below the area of the plate that is farthest from the long guide bars. Put on your ear plugs and dust mask and plow forth. Then flip the plate, and again align the long guide bars. But this time align the plate so that there is a uniform distance from the bottom side of the plate to the top of the guide bars. This ensures that the planing done on the second side will be parallel to that done on the first. By adjusting the depth of the router on the cut on the second side, you can adjust the final thickness of the plate.

No, it's not one hundred percent precise. My slabs come out fairly flat and straight but not perfect. If you want a perfectly flat top, get out your hand planes after the top is all assembled and get crackin'. Use winding sticks to show you where to reduce the surface.

Align the top surfaces of the plates with dowels, located with a doweling jig. Use four or five dowels along each joint, and glue the dowels into only one of the two holes, so the plates can be disassembled.

Use a 1" Forstner bit to enlarge the holes for the threaded rod at the front and rear of the whole slab. Start these holes using a guide as described in chapter fifteen. These larger holes allow the nuts and washers on the rod to be recessed within the top.

Secure the top to the upper rails with two lag bolts at the front of the rails, and a sliding keeper at the rear. The sliding keeper allows the top to expand and contract with moisture variations through the year. Which raises an interesting question—what will happen to the threaded rod as the wood expands? The wood by the washers will crush, and the rod itself may stretch. Check the nuts from time to time, and tighten them as necessary.

# 18 MAKING WOODEN VISES

You'll find tail vises on many traditional benches because of their versatility. One advantage they have over front vises is that there are no support members directly below the jaws, so that a long board will fit vertically in the jaw center where holding pressure is best. Also, the vise jaw and bench top can be fitted with slots for bench dogs, which let you hold long or short boards as shown in the top photo on page 66.

Wooden screws are not hard to make with the screw boxes and taps available from tool suppliers (see the list of suppliers at the end of the book), and you'll save some money since boxes and taps are cheaper than steel screws. Wooden screws will hold up well for a long time, and can apply more than enough pressure for your needs. However, you do need a lathe to make a round shaft for the threads and a drill press to accurately align the threaded hole. If you prefer, steel screws can be fitted onto either of the two vises described here.

## Tail Vise

Before you build your tail vise, take a close look at how it's designed so you'll understand where the forces are transferred when the vise clamps down on work. You'll be better able to build a functional vise when you understand the purpose of each part.

The moving jaw pushes your work against the

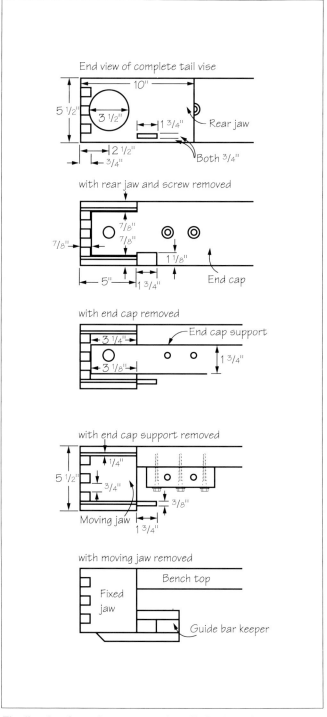

The five drawings above present the tail vise in various progressive cross sections to show how parts fit together. Understand how all the parts work before building this vise.

## MATERIALS LIST

| Part | | Dimension |
|------|------|-----------|
| A | Jaws (fixed and moving) (2) | $1\frac{3}{4}" \times 5\frac{1}{2}" \times 5"$ |
| B | Moving jaw | $1\frac{3}{4}" \times 5\frac{1}{2}" \times 6\frac{3}{4}"$ |
| C | Rear jaw | $1\frac{3}{4}" \times 5\frac{1}{2}" \times 12"$ |
| D | End cap | $1\frac{3}{4}" \times 5\frac{1}{2}" \times 36"$ |
| E | End cap support | $1\frac{3}{4}" \times 2\frac{1}{2}"$ |
| F | Front of bench front section | $1\frac{3}{4}" \times 5\frac{1}{2}" \times 70"$ |
| G | Guide bar | $1\frac{1}{8}" \times 1\frac{3}{4}" \times 32"$ |
| H | Front plate | $\frac{3}{4}" \times 3\frac{3}{4}" \times 15\frac{3}{4}"$ |
| I | Top and bottom plates (2) | $\frac{3}{4}" \times 5" \times 13"$ |

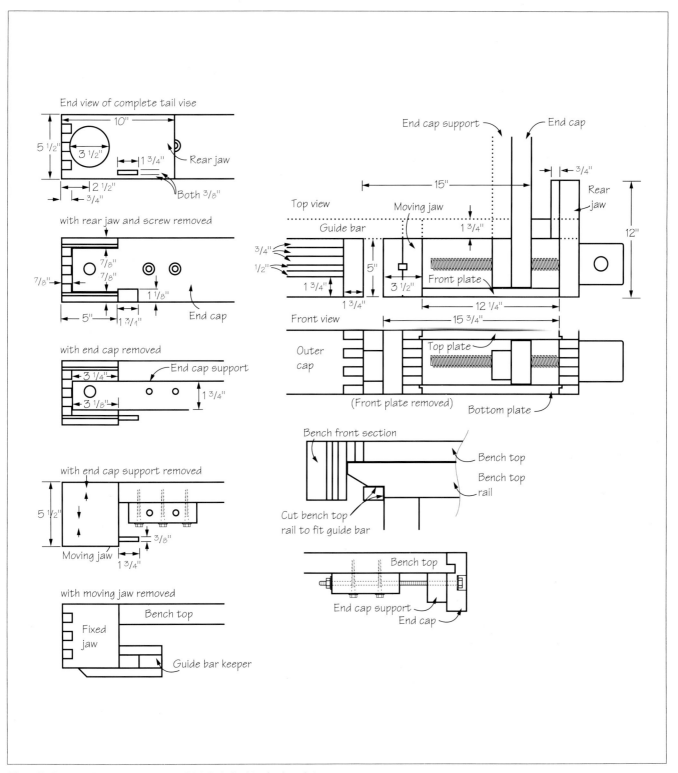

*The tail vise attaches to an end cap which is bolted to the bench top.*

fixed jaw. The screw, however, does not directly push against the moving jaw. If it did, the end of the screw would eventually bore a hole into the back of the moving jaw. So the moving jaw gets pushed by the rear jaw, which in turn gets pushed by the knuckle of the screw. Because the rear jaw pushes the moving jaw, it is very important to have a solid connection between the two. The outer plate, top and bottom plates, and guide bar all transfer force from the rear to the moving jaw, and must be joined with care for a tight fit.

The screw knuckle shoulder pushes the rear jaw by pulling against the screw threads. These threads pull against their corresponding threads within the end

*A tail vise gives two very useful clamping alternatives. Long work can be placed vertically in the jaws since there are no vise parts below the jaws to interfere. Or, work can be held on top of the bench with dogs, one of which fits in the vise and the other in the bench top.*

*Use a drift pin and large washer to secure the screw to the rear jaw, so that as the screw is opened, the jaws will come with it.*

cap. As the vise clamps down on work, it pulls the end cap away from the bench. Threaded rods hold the cap firmly against the end of the bench. A heavy block, lag screwed to the underside of the bench top, connects the threaded rods to the bench top.

But that doesn't complete the chain of force transfer on this particular bench design, which has the bench top in four sections so that it can be easily disassembled. The first of these sections contains the fixed jaw, but the threaded rods are attached to the second of the four. These two sections must be securely fixed together, or else as the vise is tightened it will push the first away from the second, shearing along the edges where they join. A dozen or so ½" dowels installed along this joint hold the two together and complete the circle of forces between the two jaws.

Begin building the tail vise by cutting out all your parts to size as shown on the list. Choose straight pieces for these parts. Set up a finger joint jig at the table saw as described in chapter six, using a dado set stacked out to ¾" wide. Use this setup to cut finger joints in the fixed, moving and rear jaws, as well as the outer cap that joins the fixed jaw, and the front plate that joins the moving and rear jaws.

Note that this front plate is ¾" thick, whereas the jaws it joins are both 1¾" thick. This means you must alter the height of the dado to accommodate the thickness of the joining part. Also note that the front plate does not align flush to the top or bottom of the jaws, but is inset ¾" both at top and bottom. The top and bottom plates, both ¾" thick, slide in above and below the front plate to take this up. Thus, make the front plate with fingers on its outer edges as shown (rather than slots), and make the jaws with fingers on the outer edges too.

Make the moving jaw out of two pieces of 1¾" stock. Put finger joints into only one of the two. Cut a bench dog dado along the inside face of each of these on the table saw with multiple cuts. The exact dimensions of the dado will depend on the size of the dogs you use. Get them first so you can make test dadoes in scrap to determine the exact size. Fit the dado so the dog will slide easily within but will stay up by itself without dropping from gravity. Don't glue the two jaw pieces together yet.

Cut ¼"×¼" dadoes along the inside faces of the moving and rear jaws for the tongues of the top and bottom plates. Position the inner edges of these dadoes at ¾" from the outer edges of the jaws. Stop the dadoes on the rear jaw so that they are no longer than 5". Make these stopped cuts on the table saw by measuring 5" from the front of the blade toward the back of the table, and draw a line on the table. Make multiple cuts with the saw, adjusting the fence to establish the width of the dadoes. During each cut, push the rear jaw only as far as the 5" line, then pull it back. Use the same setups for the moving jaw, stopping the cut at 5" along the bottom of the jaw, but going through at the top. Use a ¼" chisel to complete the stopped dadoes, which will be rounded on the ends from the blade.

Cut ⅜"×1¾" mortises on the rear jaw to fit the guide bar, and on the guide bar for the moving jaw. Use a mortising chisel on the drill press (chapter sixteen) to cut the mortises, or bore holes with the drill press or dowel jig and chisel the mortises square.

Cut tenons on the guide bar and moving jaw to fit the mortises. Cut the tenon on the jaw using your table saw cutoff box as a guide. Place the box on the table saw, and raise the blade to 1¾" above the box plywood. Mark out the inside end of the jaw to show where the tenon will go. Place the jaw on end against the fence of the box, and cut the waste away from either side of the tenon. Then make more cuts toward the top of the jaw to remove some of the waste from that area. Don't remove all the waste, because you need some to support the part as it is cut. Leave ¼" or so at the end, then cut that off with a handsaw. Cut a tenon on the end of the guide bar with the table saw tenoning jig (chapter three).

Bore a hole in the rear jaw for the screw shank. The diameter you use will depend on the screw box you use (or size of steel screw), since the box will work only with one diameter shaft. Glue together the rear and moving jaws with the guide bar and front plate as in photo 1 (page 68).

Make a turning blank for the screw by gluing together blocks for the knuckle as in photo 2 (page 68). Let it dry thoroughly, then turn the shaft down to the exact diameter specified by the instructions that come with the screw box. Use the box to cut the threads as in photo 3 (page 68).

Make the end cap out of two pieces as shown in the drawings. Cut a groove along the inside edge of the outer piece, to fit a tongue on the edge of the bench top itself. Make this tongue along the bench top edge with a router and a straight flute bit. Clamp a fence to the top to guide the router and limit its cut. Bore a hole in the end cap on the drill press for the screw to fit. Take extra care that this hole is bored at 90°. Tap the hole for threads as in photo 8 (page 69).

Laminate pieces together for the front bench section, much as you did for the other sections as described in chapter seventeen. However, this front section differs from the others in several respects: It is

*A front vise is very simple to make and handy for many tasks.*

*Use a drift pin and washer as shown to secure the screw to the vise jaw. Screw on spacers inside the jaw to provide room for the washer and drift pin.*

*Photo 1—Glue together the moving jaw, rear jaw, guide bar, and front plate of the tail vise. Ensure that the four pieces are square to each other.*

*Photo 2—Glue up a turning blank out of hardwood for the vise screw. Be sure all parts are of equal thicknesses, and are square, so that all surfaces contact for a solid glue bond.*

*Photo 3—Turn the blank on a lathe to the exact diameter specified in the instructions with your thread-cutting tool. Make a test blank and sample threads, then cut your vise screw threads.*

much thicker, not as wide, and has the fixed jaw with its finger joint. Bore holes into the layers for threaded rods that will hold all the top sections together, as described in chapter seventeen.

Incorporate bench dog slots into these laminations by spacing short pieces closely together as in photo 4 (page 69). Ensure that the pieces are uniformly spaced by making a spacer that you place between them as they are positioned on the lamination. Nail down each section in its proper location during the glue up, then glue and clamp the remaining pieces.

Glue the front of the moving jaw to the inside moving jaw, taking care to align the two dadoes for the dog slot. Join the front bench section to the other sections with a dozen dowels as discussed above, then bolt together all the bench top sections and turn them upside down. Fix the end cap onto the end with short threaded rod sections as in photo 5 (page 69). Put the tail vise in place as shown in the photo.

The tail vise is held in place by two keepers on the guide bar, as well as by the screw itself. Install the screw and keepers as shown in photo 6 (page 69). Cut tongues on the ends of the top and bottom plates at the table saw, and slide them into place within their dadoes on the moving and rear jaws. Hold the plates in place at each end with one small screw, which comes from the top or bottom of the jaw and contacts the plate tenon within its groove.

Mount the bench top onto the leg assembly with the right top rail just to the left of the fixed jaw. Let the guide bar come close to the front edge of the front right post. You will have to cut off about ¾" from the bottom of the front end of the top rail to make way for the guide rail, as shown in the drawing.

## Front Vise

After making the tail vise, a front vise will be simple. Remove the front bench top section, and cut grooves

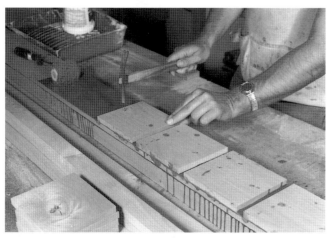

*Photo 4—Laminate together a front section for the bench, incorporating within this section slots for bench dogs. Nail the short parts between slots in place during the glue up to hold them steady while clamped.*

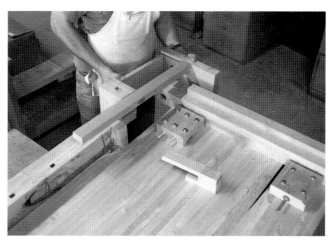

*Photo 5—Fit the tail vise to the bench top with the top pieces bolted together and the whole top placed upside down. Check that the guide bar slides easily in its notch in the end cap.*

*Photo 6—Install the screw in the vise. Check that the jaws slide easily as the screw is turned, and install keepers as shown to hold the vise in place.*

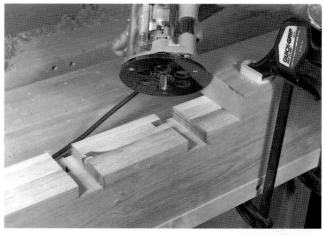

*Photo 7—Cut slots for front vise guides on the bottom of the front section of the bench. Use a straight bit in the router, guide the cut with a fence clamped to the piece that the router base rubs on.*

in the bottom of it for guides with a router and straight flute bit. Clamp a fence to the underside of the work to guide the router during the cut. Rub the router base against the edge of the fence as shown in photo 7. Bore a hole for the screw, and tap it as in photo 8. Join the guides to the jaw with mortise and tenon joints, much as you joined the guide bar for the tail vise. When the guides are in place, screw a keeper over them to hold them in place.

*Photo 8—Cut internal threads for the screw in the front section of the bench top.*

# 19 WORKBENCH ON CABINET OF DRAWERS

**A**long with the large number of parts that make up the carcass frames, you'll need a lot of ¼" plywood for this project. If you can afford it, use good quality Baltic birch or similar plywood. But cheaper grades will suffice. Some hardwood plywoods come in 5' square sheets as well as 4×8. Determine which size you will use, then make drawings of such sheets with the parts you need drawn in with dimensions. Carefully figure the most efficient way to cut the pieces you need, then determine the number you need to buy.

Begin by getting out all the parts, but leave the

*This workbench combines storage with a sturdy bench top, and is a good choice if you have room for only one piece of shop furniture.*

drawer parts over-width for now, and rip them to final width after the carcasses are assembled so you can cut them to fit. Choose straight pieces for the drawer frame components, because bowed or warped pieces will cause the drawers to bind. Slightly distorted pieces on the side frames will work, because you will pull them straight when you glue up the carcasses.

*Construct the drawers with a locking groove joint as shown here, or use dovetails.*

*Build spacer trestles for the bench top to sit on. Join the cross pieces to the trestle with dadoes cut into both the cross pieces and the trestle top.*

Cut open mortise and tenon joints on all the side frame pieces and the double carcass center frame using a table saw tenoning jig as in chapter seven. Make the tenon thickness approximately $^{5}/_{16}$", and the mortises to match. However, while the length of the tenons on the side frame rails matches the width of the vertical frame pieces they join, the same isn't true for the mortises. Cut the mortises $1^{3}/_{4}$" deep, rather than the full 2" width of the tenons. The reason for this is that the width of the tenons will be reduced by a $^{1}/_{4}$" groove that holds the plywood panel in the side frames. This doesn't apply to the double carcass center frame, which has no panel. Make those mortises a full 2" deep.

Once the mortises and tenons are cut, make the panel groove in the side frame parts on the table saw with your regular blade as in the photo at right. Cut the groove in two passes, alternately placing each side of the part against the fence. Carefully adjust the fence-to-blade distance so that the resulting groove provides a snug, but not too tight, fit for the plywood panels.

Bore $^{3}/_{8}$" holes in the vertical side frame parts for the dowels that will join the side frames and the drawer frames. Do the same for the double carcass center frame. Center these holes along the part width, and make them $^{5}/_{8}$" deep on the side frames, all the way through for the center frame. Note that the alignment of these holes establishes the distance between drawer frames, and must be accurate so the

*Photo 1—Cut a groove along the inside edge of the side frame parts at the table saw.*

drawers will fit well. Don't yet bore the holes at the ends of the vertical side frame parts for the carcass rails.

Cut out the plywood panels for the side frames, and glue up the frames as shown in photo 2 (page 74).

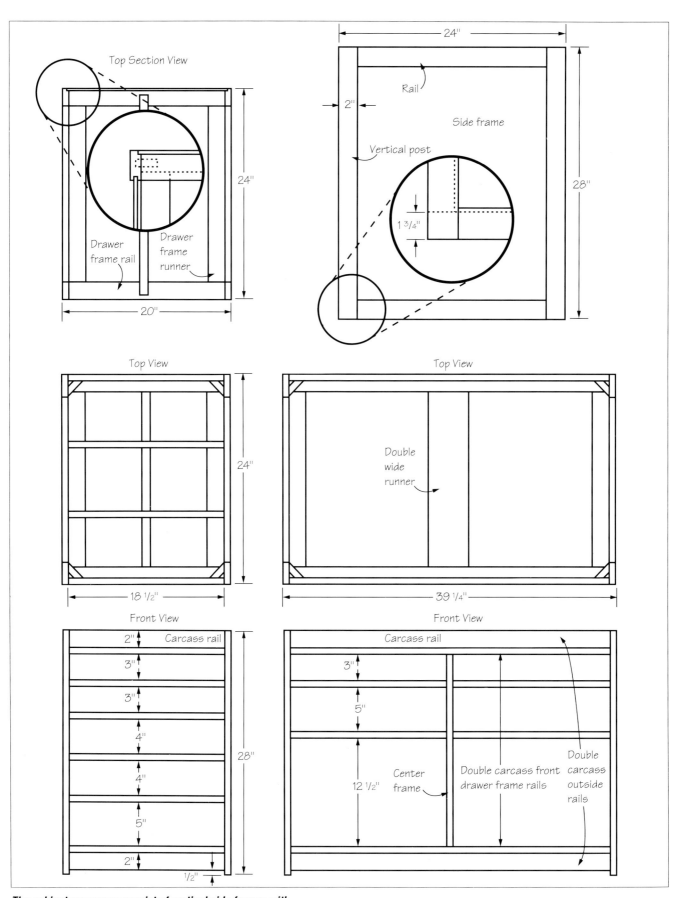

**Top Section View**

Drawer frame rail

Drawer frame runner

24"

20"

24"

Rail

2"

Side frame

Vertical post

1 3/4"

28"

**Top View**

24"

18 1/2"

**Top View**

Double wide runner

39 1/4"

**Front View**

2" Carcass rail

3"

3"

4"

4"

5"

2"

1/2"

28"

**Front View**

Carcass rail

3"

5"

12 1/2"

Center frame

Double carcass front drawer frame rails

Double carcass outside rails

*The cabinet carcasses consist of vertical side frames with horizontal drawer frames and rails located between them. The double cabinet also has a central vertical divider.*

# MATERIALS LIST

| Part | | Dimension |
|---|---|---|
| A | Side frame vertical posts (8) | $\frac{3}{4}$" × 2" × 28" |
| B | Side and center frame rails (10) | $\frac{3}{4}$" × 2" × 24" |
| C | Drawer frame front rails, and top and bottom outside rails (14) | $\frac{3}{4}$" × 2" × 18$\frac{1}{2}$" |
| D | Drawer frame rear rails, and top mid rails (12) | $\frac{3}{4}$" × 1$\frac{3}{4}$" × 18$\frac{1}{2}$" |
| E | Drawer frame side rails (24) | $\frac{3}{4}$" × 2" × 21" |
| F | Drawer frame guides (11) | $\frac{1}{2}$" × 1" × 23" |
| G | Double carcass front drawer frame and outside rails (6) | $\frac{3}{4}$" × 2" × 37$\frac{3}{4}$" |
| H | Double carcass rear drawer frame and top mid rails (4) | $\frac{3}{4}$" × 1$\frac{3}{4}$" × 37$\frac{3}{4}$" |
| I | Center frame posts (2) | $\frac{3}{4}$" × 2" × 22" |
| J | Double drawer frame centers (2) | $\frac{3}{4}$" × 4$\frac{3}{4}$" × 21" |
| K | Drawer fronts (4) | $\frac{3}{4}$" × 3" × 18$\frac{3}{8}$" |
| L | Drawer fronts (2) | $\frac{3}{4}$" × 4" × 18$\frac{3}{8}$" |
| M | Drawer fronts (3) | $\frac{3}{4}$" × 5" × 18$\frac{3}{8}$" |
| N | Drawer fronts (2) | $\frac{3}{4}$" × 12$\frac{1}{2}$" × 18$\frac{3}{8}$" |
| O | Drawer sides (8) | $\frac{1}{2}$" × 3" × 22$\frac{3}{4}$" |
| P | Drawer sides (4) | $\frac{1}{2}$" × 4" × 22$\frac{3}{4}$" |
| Q | Drawer sides (6) | $\frac{1}{2}$" × 5" × 22$\frac{3}{4}$" |
| R | Drawer sides (4) | $\frac{1}{2}$" × 12$\frac{1}{2}$" × 22$\frac{3}{4}$" |
| S | Drawer backs (4) | $\frac{1}{2}$" × 3" × 17$\frac{7}{8}$" |
| T | Drawer backs (2) | $\frac{1}{2}$" × 4" × 17$\frac{7}{8}$" |
| U | Drawer backs (3) | $\frac{1}{2}$" × 5" × 17$\frac{7}{8}$" |
| V | Drawer backs (2) | $\frac{1}{2}$" × 12$\frac{1}{2}$" × 17$\frac{7}{8}$" |
| W | Drawer guides (11) | $\frac{1}{2}$" × 2" × 22$\frac{3}{8}$" |
| X | Plywood drawer bottoms (11) | $\frac{1}{4}$" × 17$\frac{7}{8}$" × 21$\frac{3}{4}$" |
| Y | Plywood sides (4) | $\frac{1}{4}$" × 20$\frac{1}{2}$" × 24$\frac{1}{2}$" |
| Z | Plywood back, single carcass | $\frac{1}{4}$" × 19$\frac{1}{4}$" × 24$\frac{1}{4}$" |
| AA | Plywood back, double carcass | $\frac{1}{4}$" × 24$\frac{1}{4}$" × 38$\frac{1}{2}$" |
| BB | Plywood top, single carcass | $\frac{1}{4}$" × 19$\frac{1}{4}$" × 23$\frac{1}{4}$" |
| CC | Plywood top, double carcass | $\frac{1}{4}$" × 23$\frac{1}{4}$" × 38$\frac{1}{2}$" |

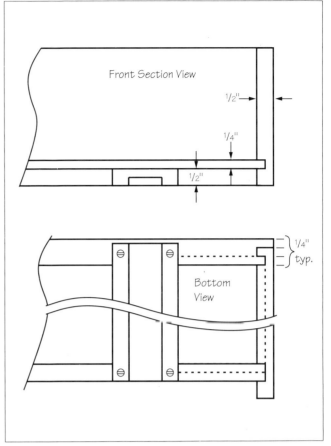

**All the joinery for the drawers can be done on the table saw, except the mortise for the drawer guide, which you make with a router and template guide.**

Pull them together with bar clamps, and check the frame for squareness by measuring diagonally across opposing corners. When these distances are equal, the frame is square. Then put C-clamps with clamp blocks on the joints to pull the mortises onto the tenons. Once the C-clamps are in place, remove the bar clamps.

When the frames are out of clamps, set up at the drill press to bore $\frac{5}{8}$"-deep holes for the top and bottom rails, as in photo 3 (page 74). Position the top holes at $\frac{3}{8}$" on center from the side edge of the frame, and at $\frac{1}{2}$" and 1$\frac{1}{4}$" on center from the top edge of the frame. Add $\frac{1}{2}$" to the last two dimensions to locate the dowel holes on the bottoms of the frames. Note that these locations place the holes so their corresponding holes on the rails will be away from the internal edges. Later you will cut a rabbet in the rear rails for the rear plywood piece to fit into, and the dowels in these rails must be located away from that rabbet.

Also bore holes in the middle of the top rails on the side frames for mid rails that provide support for the plywood top in the middle of the carcass. Place these rails $\frac{1}{4}$" below the top of the side frames to make way for the plywood top piece.

Cut grooves and stub tenons in the drawer frame parts at the table saw. First cut grooves along the entire length of the inside edge of the front and rear drawer frame rails, much as you did for the panel grooves in the side frames. But make these grooves $\frac{5}{16}$" wide and $\frac{1}{2}$" deep. Then cut tenons to match on the runners, or side pieces of the drawer frames, using the tenoning jig at the table saw. Note that the double carcass has two double-wide drawer frames, one at the top and one below. Each of these has one extra wide runner in the middle.

Before you glue up the drawer frames, cut mortises in the front and rear rails to fit the drawer guides. Cut these mortises with a router and a specially made template, as described in chapter thirteen. Make these mortises 1"×¼", and center them accurately on the rails.

Glue up the drawer frames, just as you did with the side frames. C-clamps with clamp blocks on the joints are important to pull the slot mortise walls onto the tenons. Make the drawer guides that fit in the mortises. Round the corners on these pieces with a power sander so they will fit in the rounded mortises left by your router, or square the corners of the mortises to fit the guides. Screw the guides into the frames as in photo 4 at bottom.

When the drawer frames are out of clamps, use a doweling jig to bore dowel holes in ends of the front and rear rails to join these frames to the side frames. Carefully regulate the depth of these holes so that when your dowels are placed within them, the remaining length of dowel will be just shorter than the length of the hole in the side frame. The joints should appear as in photo 5 (page 75). Also bore similar holes to join the double carcass center frame to the double-wide drawer frames it contacts.

Dry fit and clamp the side frames with the four outside top and bottom rails, but without the drawer frames or top and bottom mid rails. Use ½"-long dowels to locate the rails, and hold it all together with bar clamps. Now cut a ¼"×¼" rabbet for the plywood top and back along the inside edges of the parts. Do this with a bearing guided rabbeting bit in a router. Square the corners of the rabbets with a chisel.

Before gluing up the carcasses, screw the top and bottom drawer frames to the adjacent top and bottom rails. You can't do this after the carcass is assembled because the other drawer frames are in the way. Use brown glue, or urea formaldehyde, to glue up these carcasses. This glue has a very long open time, and will not begin to "grab" the parts half way through the glue up. There are a lot of parts to glue here and it will take a lot of time, and yellow glue (aliphatic resin) will grab before you can get it together. Yellow glue, however, is appropriate for the remainder of the project.

Glue the parts, assemble the carcasses, and clamp up as in photo 6 (page 75). Carefully check for squareness on the front and back as well as on the top and bottom. Notice that where you place the clamps will affect the squareness. Fuss and fudge until it's square, then clean up the glue with hot water.

Install glue blocks in the corners of the carcass as in photo 7 (page 75). Give the end grain of the blocks time to absorb the glue, and secure them with screws. These blocks will significantly add to the overall strength of the box.

**Photo 2—Glue up the side frames by pulling them together with bar clamps, then put C-clamps with clamp blocks onto the mortise and tenon joints.**

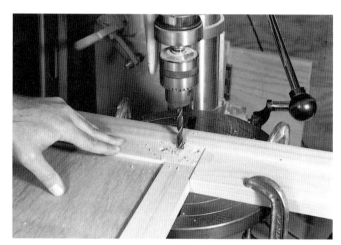

**Photo 3—After the side frames are out of clamps, bore dowel holes in the corners to join the front and rear rails.**

**Photo 4—Glue up the drawer frames, and screw the drawer guides into their mortises on the front and rear drawer frame rails.**

When the carcasses are out of clamps, carefully measure the heights between the drawer frames. Determine the exact widths for your drawer parts by taking these dimensions and subtracting just enough clearance to allow for expansion of the drawer parts. On the smaller drawers, subtract $\frac{1}{16}$", and on the medium ones subtract just under $\frac{1}{8}$", on the widest a full $\frac{1}{8}$".

To join the drawer parts, you can use one of the dovetail jigs described in chapter eleven or sixteen. If you do use one of these jigs, you will need to alter the lengths of the parts to match the dimensions of the dovetails you use. (The given dimensions are for making drawers using a locking groove joint cut at the table saw with a dado set.) This joint is ultimately not as strong as dovetails, but it will hold up well, does not require a dovetail jig, and is much faster to make than dovetails—even with a jig.

Set up a $\frac{1}{4}$" dado in the table saw. Raise it to $\frac{1}{4}$" above the table, and set the fence the same distance from the blade. Cut this dado into the inside front edge of the drawer sides as in photo 8 (page 76). Next raise the blade to $\frac{1}{2}$", leave the fence in place, and cut a dado into the end of the drawer fronts as in photo 9 (page 76), with the inside of the drawer front to the fence. Next remove the dado, replace your combination blade, raise it to $\frac{5}{16}$", and set the fence $\frac{1}{4}$" from the outside of the blade. Place the drawer fronts flat on the table inside facedown as in photo 10 (page 76), and cut off the tongue as shown. Try this joint with test pieces to see how it fits, then set up to do the drawers.

To join the drawer rears to the sides, use a dado cut in the sides as shown in the drawing on page 73. Cut a groove along the bottom of all the drawer parts for the plywood bottom. Cut the groove at $\frac{1}{2}$" above the drawer part bottoms. Mortise the drawer fronts and rears for the guides, as you did with the drawer frames. Glue up the drawers, and install screws through the sides into the front and rear. Check for squareness, and then screw down the guides.

Install the drawers, and set their fronts flush with the fronts of the cabinets. Screw in stop blocks at the rear of the cabinets on the inside of the side frames to limit the travel of the drawers. Now cut out plywood panels to fit the top and back, and nail them in place with small finish nails placed every 4" or so. Don't use glue on these panels, so they can be easily removed if necessary.

Follow the instructions in chapter seventeen for laminating a bench top together, and install whatever vises you choose, using instructions from chapters eighteen and twenty-one. Suspend the bench top

*Photo 5—Join the drawer frames to the side frames with dowels. Bore the holes deep enough so the dowels won't be "too long."*

*Photo 6—Glue up the carcasses using brown glue, which has a long open time. Use a lot of clamps with a little pressure, rather than just a few pressing hard.*

*Photo 7—Install glue blocks at the eight main corners of each carcass. Carefully predrill for the screws so the blocks won't split.*

Photo 8—Begin the locking groove joint for the drawer fronts with a groove in the drawer sides at the front along the inside.

Photo 9—Next raise the same cutter to make a deeper groove along the end of the drawer front.

Photo 10—Finally trim the inside tongues on the ends of the drawer fronts. The resulting shortened tongue fits in the groove cut in the drawer side.

above the carcasses with heavy spacers as shown in the color photo. Join the short cross pieces with dadoes in both the cross pieces and longer spacers. This is a good place to use up big heavy chunks of hardwood that have defects. When locating the bench top, first position the cabinets, then place the spacers on them and screw these to the top rails of the cabinets. Place the top on the spacers, and inspect underneath to see that the top contacts the spacers everywhere. If not, use door shims to take up the difference where there are gaps (due to uneven floors), then screw the spacers securely to the top from below.

# 20 GRINDER CABINET

This cabinet uses the same basic joinery techniques as the workbench on cabinet of drawers, so if you want to make both, it's best to make them simultaneously. Doing so lets you run all the common joinery setups at the same time so you don't end up doing them twice. There are, however, a few differences between the two projects, and I outline those here. If you want to make the grinder cabinet alone, first read the instructions in the previous chapter to get the necessary details on the setups required.

You'll need four rather long vertical posts for the corners. You may have some trouble finding parts that are flat along their face to use here, but slightly distorted parts will work OK. This is because they will be glued to so many other parts that they will straighten out along their faces. However, the edges of the parts must be straight. You can accomplish that with the straightedge jig discussed earlier. The drawer frame components must be straight along their face, otherwise the drawers will bind.

Begin the joinery with the four middle through mortises in the four vertical posts. These mortises join the mid rails in the side frames to the posts. There are several ways to cut the four middle mortises. A chisel mortise on the drill press will cut square mortises in one operation. The router mortising jig shown earlier will also do the job, though you'll need to make two cuts for each mortise—one on each side to cut the mortise all the way through.

A third way is to bore out the bulk at the drill press (or with a doweling jig) and then square them up with a chisel, as shown in photo 1 on page 78. Set up on the drill press as explained in chapter fifteen. Mark on the parts the top and bottom of the mortise. With a $5/16$" bit set to cut along the center of the parts, bore as many holes within your marks as you can. Then use chisels to square up the mortises. As you do so, look carefully within the mortise to see where the sides of the bored round holes are. Don't cut these away entirely, if you do you will expand the mortise beyond $5/16$". By following the bit marks, you will make a uniform, square mortise.

If you make the mortises as wide as the rails, you

*This grinder cabinet uses the same construction techniques as the cabinets in the previous chapter, and can be made simultaneously.*

will need to stop the rabbet and groove cuts on the rail edges for the plywood top and side panels. Better to make the mortise and tenon $1\frac{1}{2}$" wide, leaving $1/4$" on the top and bottom of the tenon. This makes cutting the rabbets and grooves easier.

Next set up on the table saw with a tenoning jig, and cut the tenons on all the side frame rails to match the width of the through mortises. Adjust the thickness of the tenons so they fit snugly in the mortises without having to be jammed in. Lastly, use the tenoning jig to cut the open mortises on the ends of the four vertical posts. Match the mortise widths with the tenon thickness.

The remainder of the carcass and drawer joinery for this cabinet is exactly the same as that described in the previous chapter, with one exception. The plywood top fits into rabbets cut into the middle rails. You can't cut these rabbets with the rails dry-fitted in place as you can for the workbench cabinets, because the posts are in the way. Therefore, cut these rabbets into the rails at the table saw or router table before you glue up the carcass. Note that the plywood top must be notched at the corners to fit around the posts. Mark out these notches and cut them with a handsaw or band saw. See photo 2 (page 79).

The purpose of the superstructure is to mount a jackshaft or mandrel on which your grinding wheels turn, with space beneath for a motor to drive it. If you have a bench grinder, which incorporates the motor and shaft in one unit, you have no need for the superstructure and might as well make the cabinet

*Photo 1—Cut through mortises on the vertical posts by boring out the bulk on the drill press, then squaring up the mortise with a chisel.*

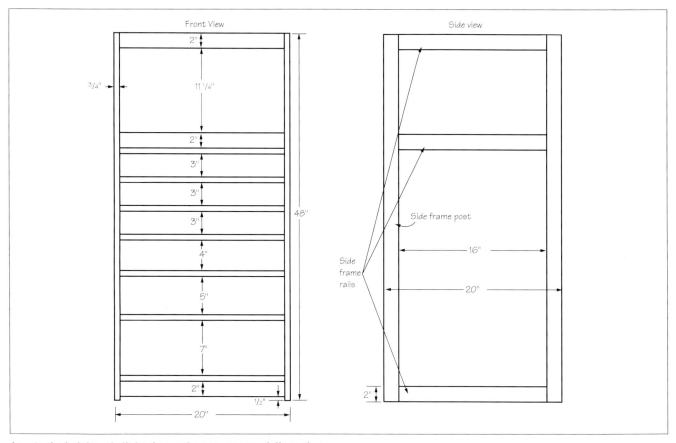

*Locate the heights of all the drawer frames very carefully so that the drawers will fit well between them.*

Photo 2—Fit the plywood top into rabbets in the mid rails, and notch them around the vertical posts. Secure the top with finish nails.

Photo 3—It's tight quarters fitting in a tool rest next to your grinding wheels. Place the rest so it can handle from 20° to 30° angles.

## MATERIALS LIST

| Part | | Dimension |
|------|------|-----------|
| A | Vertical posts (4) | ¾" × 2" × 48" |
| B | Side rails (6) | ¾" × 2" × 20" |
| C | Drawer frame front rails and outside carcass rails (13) | ¾" × 2" × 18½" |
| D | Drawer frame rear rails and top mid rails (9) | ¾" × 1¾" × 18½" |
| E | Drawer frame side rails (14) | ¾" × 2" × 17" |
| F | Runners (6) | ½" × 1" × 19" |
| G | Runner guides (6) | ½" × 2" × 18⅜" |
| H | Drawer fronts (3) | ¾" × 3" × 18⅜" |
| I | Drawer front | ¾" × 4" × 18⅜" |
| J | Drawer front | ¾" × 5" × 18⅜" |
| K | Drawer front | ¾" × 7¼" × 18⅜" |
| L | Drawer backs (3) | ½" × 3" × 17⅞" |
| M | Drawer back | ½" × 4" × 17⅞" |
| N | Drawer back | ½" × 5" × 17⅞" |
| O | Drawer back | ½" × 7¼" × 17⅞" |
| P | Drawer sides (6) | ½" × 3" × 18¾" |
| Q | Drawer sides (2) | ½" × 4" × 18¾" |
| R | Drawer sides (2) | ½" × 5" × 18¾" |
| S | Drawer sides (2) | ½" × 7¼" × 18¾" |
| T | Plywood top | ¼" × 19¼" × 19¼" |
| U | Plywood sides (2) | ¼" × 16½" × 31½" |
| V | Plywood back | ¼" × 19¼" × 31¼" |
| W | Drawer bottoms (6) | ¼" × 17¾" × 17⅞" |

without it and just install the bench grinder on top. If you have no bench grinder, but you do have an old motor lying around, the cheaper route is to get a mandrel and some wheels and set up as shown.

Mandrels and wheels are available at hardware stores or through the mail. See the suppliers list in the back of the book. The best type of grinding wheel to use for woodworking tools is vitrified aluminum oxide. Vitrified refers to the bonding agent that holds together the abrasive grit, which in this case is aluminum oxide. Two other variables are bond grade and structure, which basically tell you how much grit is in the wheel and the wheel's overall density. Get wheels in the medium range for both these factors.

Wheels 6" in diameter and 1" wide are inexpensive and will allow you to put a hollow grind on your chisel bevels.

However you set up your grinder, know the maxi-

mum recommended rpm for your wheels, and don't run them faster. The danger is that the wheels will fly apart. Whenever you start a grinder, step aside just in case something accidentally hit the wheel while you weren't looking and it cracked and is now about to fly apart. Always wear goggles when grinding.

Build a tool rest like the one shown in photo 3 (bottom left). Don't try to grind anything on the wheels without a rest. Mount it with a pivot so you can change the angle to suit the bevel of the tool you are sharpening.

Be aware that the fine metal dust that results from grinding is hazardous to your woodworking. If it gets on your wood and the wood gets wet (as when you wet sand), dark rust spots will appear on the wood. Keep the grinder in a far corner, or clean up carefully after using it.

# 21 INSTALLING METAL VISES

**R**eady-made steel and cast iron vises have several advantages over wooden vises. They are more rigid, and so the jaws will keep closer to parallel when in use. Some have a quick release feature that allows you to release the screw threads and open the jaws to large sizes without having to spin the screw. I would not say, however, that iron vises necessarily last longer than wood; many old wooden screws exist and are still in use.

One potential problem with an iron vise is that you might accidentally hit the iron with a chisel or other tool, nicking the tool edge. For that reason, it is best to mount the vise so that as little of the iron is exposed as possible. Installing wooden jaws within the iron jaws accomplishes this. It also gives a softer surface for gripping your work, reducing the chance of the jaws indenting the surface of your stock.

Refer to the drawing to see how that vise is mounted with respect to the bench top. Note that the jaws are slightly lower than the top, and the fixed iron jaw is inset within it. The fixed wooden jaw butts against the bench top edge. This arrangement entirely hides the rear iron jaw and lowers the front iron jaw so that it is not as easy to hit with a tool.

Use spacers beneath the bench top to mount the vise onto it. Find a combination of spacers that will place the top of the iron jaws about ⅜" below the bench top. Turn the bench top upside down, and place the spacers and the vise on it in the location you desire. Mark on the edge of the top where the sides of the rear iron jaw intersect, then remove the vise and spacers.

Mount a straight flute bit in your router, and clamp a fence onto the bottom of the bench to guide the router while cutting a rabbet for the rear iron jaw as in photo 1 (page 81). Position the fence so that when the router base edge rubs it, the cutter makes a rabbet that equals the thickness of the rear iron jaw. Set the depth of the cut according to the spacers you chose for mounting the vise.

Take light passes with the router bit to gradually cut out the rabbet, until your router base hits the

*Iron vises are very rigid and easy to install. Many, such as this one, have quick release mechanisms that allow you to open the vise without turning the screw twenty times.*

fence. Stay between your marked lines on the bench top edge. Use a chisel to square up the corners of the rabbet.

Use lag bolts to mount the vise to the bench. Bore holes through the spacers wide enough for the lags to slide through with no resistance. Bore smaller holes in the bench for the lag threads to grip within. In most woods, the diameter of these second holes should equal the diameter of the lag shank within the threads.

Make wooden jaws out of whatever wood you like. A hardwood like oak will last a long time, but may dent softer woods. Pine jaws won't hold up as long, but will not dent most stock.

*Photo 1—Cut a rabbet in the underside of your bench top's front edge to set the rear steel jaw of the vise into. Make the cut with a straight flute bit in the router. Regulate the width of cut with a fence, which the router base rubs against.*

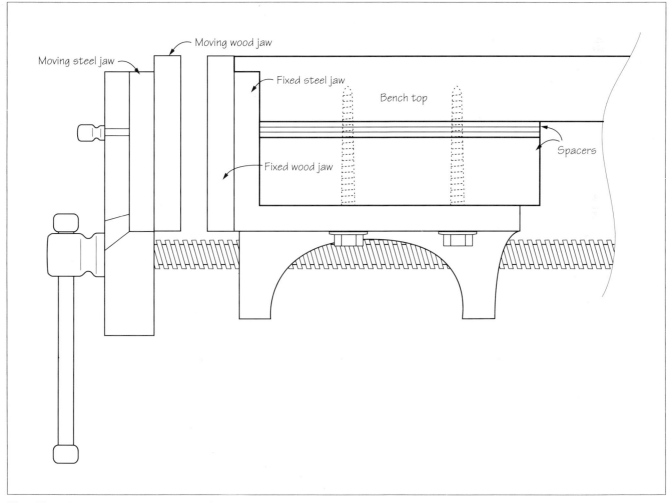

*The object of mounting a metal vise is to hide the metal with wood so that it is harder to hit the metal and dull your sharp tools. Set the fixed jaw in a rabbet in the leading edge of the bench, and attach wooden jaws to the iron ones.*

# 22 EASY-TO-MAKE SHOP CABINETS

These plywood cabinets are a good choice if you don't want to build a heavy-duty workbench, or if you want more storage and work surface in addition to another bench. The design shown here is quick to build and materials are cheap. Cabinets like these won't be as sturdy for shop purposes as more solid bench designs, but then you may not need something that sturdy if your woodworking is occasional.

Custom design the dimensions of these cabinets to fit the available space you have. Measure the length of space along the wall that you have for cabinets, then divide that number into equally spaced units of 20" to 30". Units less than 20" would be cramped, but if they're over 30", the structure will be weak since its strength depends on the sum of many parts. The lower cabinet in the drawing is roughly 5' wide and is divided into two units, although it could just as well have been divided into three.

Wall-hung cabinets must be lifted in place, so keep them small. This may mean constructing separate cabinets for each unit of length, such as the single-unit upper cabinet shown in the drawing.

Construct face frames and web frames out of solid stock. Face frames attach to the front edges of the plywood boxes. Design them so that their outer edges are flush with the outer edges of the box. Web frames are horizontal rectangles that fit in the top of the boxes, as well as in the middle to support drawers. These two types of frames add a lot of strength to the total construction. Join them with dowels as shown. Make the web frames $\frac{1}{4}$" wider than the internal width of each unit, so that the ends of the frames can fit into $\frac{1}{8}$" rabbets in the plywood.

Use $\frac{3}{4}$"-thick plywood or particleboard for the boxes. If you don't mind a rough look, get cheap construction grade plywood. For a better look, consider softwood core plywood with hardwood veneer on the outside. Paint-grade varieties of this are made with maple veneer, which looks nice stained. Use rough plywood where it's hidden and better plywood where it isn't. Carefully figure all the sizes of plywood pieces you'll need, and draw pictures of 4×8 sheets of plywood, superimposing pictures of your pieces to figure the most efficient way to use the plywood.

Rip out the plywood pieces on the table saw. See chapter fifteen on dealing with large sheets of plywood. Cut $\frac{1}{8}$" rabbets and dadoes in the edges and middle of the plywood pieces to join the various parts. See chapter nine on using a dado cutter on the table saw. Rabbets can also be cut with a router and a wide, straight flute bit. Guide the router by clamping a fence to the plywood against which the router rides. These rabbets (however made) help strengthen the structure and make it easy to assemble.

Make the back of floor-standing boxes from $\frac{1}{4}$" plywood, and make the back of wall-mounted units out of $\frac{1}{2}$" or thicker material. You will secure the wall-mounted units to the wall with screws through this plywood, so the wood needs to be strong enough to take the weight of the cabinet and its contents. The plywood also needs to be strongly secured to the cabinet sides, so install corner blocks at these joints with glue and screws after the boxes are assembled.

Assemble the boxes with glue and finish nails. First attach the web frames to the cabinet sides. Where two web frames attach at the top of one vertical divider, nail the first through the rabbet on the opposite side, and toe nail in the second from the top. Flip the assembly onto its front, then glue and nail it in the back. Flip it onto its back, and glue and nail the face frame to the exposed leading edges.

The simplest way to make doors is to cut them out of plywood. The exposed edges look kind of ratty, however, so you may choose to cover them with thin strips of solid stock glued and nailed in place. Another alternative is to make doors by edge gluing solid stock. Or, make frame and panel doors as shown in chapter twenty-three, but make them oversized to the hole and fit them over the face frames as shown in this drawing. You'll find standard kitchen cabinet hinges for this kind of mounting at any hardware store.

Study the drawer construction techniques shown in chapter nineteen. Use that method for drawers, or make them with dovetails using router techniques from chapter eleven or sixteen. Either way you'll need to install guides on the web frames for the drawers.

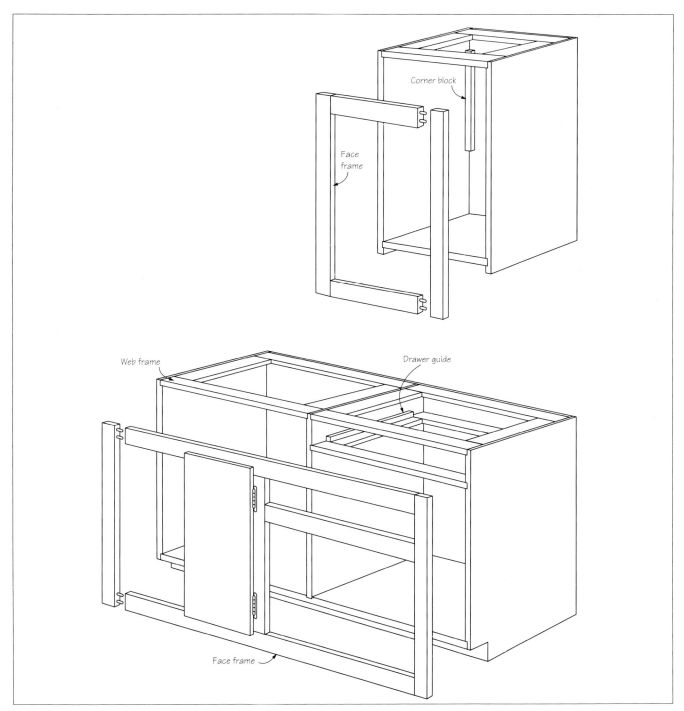

Corner block

Face
frame

Web frame

Drawer guide

Face frame

*These cabinets are much easier to make than the two benches shown earlier in the book. But plywood boxes won't hold up as long.*

The drawers can't be the same width as the internal dimension of the plywood boxes in which they fit, because the face frames are wider than the plywood. Therefore, there must be a gap between the plywood walls and the drawer sides. The guides will fill this gap and help the drawer slide smoothly. Wax from a candle helps, too. You can also use steel drawer slides, which will require special spacers to fit correctly.

You need a sturdy top if you will be attaching clamps to the edge of it for machine work. The clamps would eventually crush plywood alone. But plywood will do if all you want is an assembly table and you plan to do your machine work on another bench. For the best top, consider laminating solid stock together as explained in chapter seventeen. Screw your top to the upper web frames from below.

# 23 WALL-MOUNTED STORAGE CABINETS

uilding these storage cabinets makes use of the router mortising, tenoning and radiusing jigs from earlier chapters, and will give you a solid introduction to machining the mortise and tenon joint. Note that there are two cabinets mounted side by side in the photo. Build as many as you wish to suit your storage needs.

Begin the project by getting out the solid wood parts for the number of cabinets you want to make. If you don't have a jointer and planer to ensure that your stock is flat, choose carefully as you cut out parts. Use your straightest lumber for your door parts, otherwise the doors won't lie flush to the face frame when they are in place. Use your least flat stock for the screw blocks that attach the plywood to the frames.

Rip your parts to width and cut them to length. Note that the lengths of the rails given in the cutout list account for tenon lengths of 1½" on the side and face frames, and 1" on the doors. If you must shorten your tenons because of your tooling, shorten the rails appropriately—but don't make the tenons less than 1" long. If you don't have a router bit long enough to

*You'll learn about frame and panel construction using mortise and tenon joinery when you make these sturdy storage cabinets for the shop or house.*

make mortises at least that deep, buy one.

Mark out one of the side frame stiles (vertical frame components) for mortising. Mark on the edge of that piece the length of each mortise. Make the length of each equal to the width of the adjoining rail (horizontal frame component) with the following adjustments: subtract ½" at the top and bottom of the stile, and subtract ¼" at every internal edge of each rail. The ½" top and bottom gives the mortise walls strength on the end of the part, and the ¼" gives room for the panel groove cut into the internal edge of all frame parts.

Set up to cut the mortises with the router mortising jig (chapter ten) or with a mortising chisel at the drill press (chapter sixteen). Note that the setup you use to cut the mortises on the ends of the side frame stiles is close to the setup required to cut the mortises on the face frame and door stiles. Vary the lengths and depths of these mortises accordingly.

After you cut out all the mortises for the rail tenons, set up to cut one more mortise on the outer door stiles. Look ahead to photo 8 (page 89) to see the location and purpose of this mortise. It houses an unglued dowel that keeps the wide rail flush to the stile edge, while allowing the rail to expand and contract with moisture variations.

If you cut the mortises with the plunge router setup, you will need to square up the ends of the mortises once you are through. Keep your chisel sharp, and be careful not to increase the lengths of the mortises. Next cut the tenons using the router tenoning jig, table saw tenoning jig, or a dado set and the miter gauge as shown in previous chapters. Carefully adjust the thickness of the tenons so they fit the mortises snugly but don't split the wood around them.

Whichever tenoning setup you use, all the tenons will still need to be reduced along the top and bottom. Do so on the table saw with a dado set and the miter gauge as in photo 1 (below). Set the rip fence at a distance from the outside of the dado equal to the length of the tenon. Reduce the top of the upper rails and the bottom of the lower rails by ½", and the remaining tops and bottoms of all the rails by ¼".

The curved top rails for the doors get handled a bit differently than the rest of the rails. First cut the tenon faces on these parts just as you do for the other rails, but note that if you use the router tenoning setup you don't need to cut the tenon faces across the entire width of the part. Trim the tops of these tenons just as you did the other rails. Then put your regular blade in the table saw, and cut off the ends of the rails below the tenons as in photo 2 (page 87). Push the part only far enough to cut the waste, not the tenon. Retract the part, holding it firmly against the miter gauge. Complete these tenons by marking them out with a square, cutting with a handsaw, and paring the final surfaces with a sharp chisel.

Make a template for the curved inside edge of the door top rails using the router arcing jig shown in chapter fourteen. First, get a large sheet of scrap plywood that is bigger than one of the doors and clamp it to your bench. Draw the outside profile of one of the 16"×25" doors onto this sheet. Be sure your drawing is square. Cut a piece of plywood template stock to 8"×16". Place this piece onto the drawing at the top of the door as in photo 3 (page 87). Nail the template stock to the base plywood with small finish nails, but be sure to place the nails away from where the router cut will be made.

Mark the pivot hole on the router arcing jig at 24" from the outside of the router bit. Place a nail in the pivot hole, and drive the nail into the base plywood

*Mount the hinges flush to the edges of the face frames and doors using a router jig. The shelves sit on small holders placed in holes bored on the inside of the cabinet sides.*

*Photo 1—After cutting the tenon faces, cut their tops and bottoms on the table saw with the miter gauge and dado cutter.*

along the line of one edge of the door, as in photo 3 (page 87). Place the nail at ½" below the bottom of the drawing of the door. Make the cut.

Remove the template from the base plywood, and sand the curve. Place the template on one of the top rails. Center it on the rail along its length, and align the top edges of the rail and the template flush. Scribe the line of the curve onto the top rail. Remove the template, and cut away the waste to within ⅛" of the line with a band, scroll or saber saw. Replace the

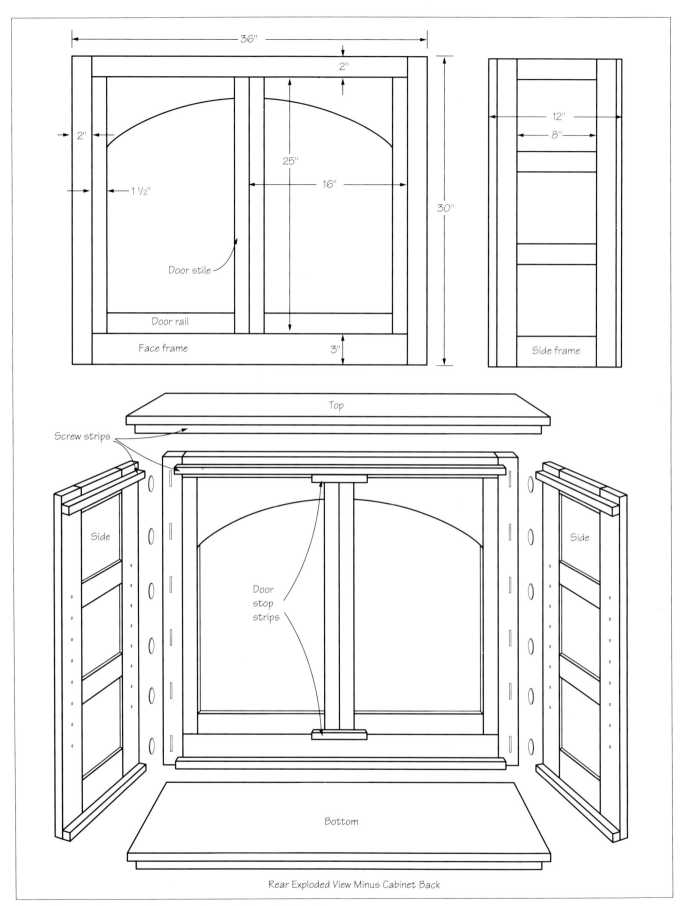

36"

2"

2"

2"

1 1/2"

25"

16"

30"

3"

12"

8"

Door stile

Door rail

Face frame

Side frame

Top

Screw strips

Side

Side

Door
stop
strips

Bottom

Rear Exploded View Minus Cabinet Back

*The cabinet top, bottom and rear are pieces of plywood joined to
the frames with screws and screw strips.*

# MATERIALS LIST

| Part | | Dimension |
|------|---|-----------|
| A | Face frame and side frame stile (6) | ¾" × 2" × 30" |
| B | Face frame top rail | ¾" × 2" × 35" |
| C | Face frame bottom rail | ¾" × 3" × 35" |
| D | Side frame rails (6) | ¾" × 2" × 11" |
| E | Side frame bottom rails (2) | ¾" × 3" × 11" |
| F | Door stiles (4) | ¾" × 1½" × 25" |
| G | Door bottom rails (2) | ¾" × 2" × 15" |
| H | Door top rails (2) | ¾" × 7" × 15" |
| I | Shelves (2) | ¾" × 11½" × 34¼" |
| J | Plywood back | ½" × 30" × 36" |
| K | Plywood top and bottom (2) | ½" × 12" × 34½" |
| L | Plywood door panels (2) | ¼" × 13½" × 23" (approx.) |
| M | Plywood side panels (6) | ¼" × 7⅜" × 8⅜" (approx.) |

*Photo 2—Cut away the area below the tenons on the door top rails using the miter gauge and your regular blade at the table saw.*

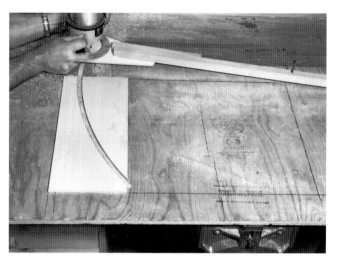

*Photo 3—Make a curved template for the door top rails with a router arcing jig. Align the template stock and the router jig to a full-scale drawing of one of the doors.*

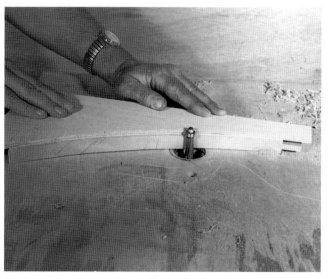

*Photo 4—Use the template to flush trim the curved edge onto the door top rails.*

template on the inside of the rail. Nail it in place with two or three small finish nails. Now flush trim the curved edge of the rail on the router table using a bearing-guided flush trim bit as in photo 4 (bottom right).

It's easier to rout door hinge mortises into the face frame stiles before the face frames are glued up. Buy hinges for your doors and make a template to match them as explained in chapter thirteen. Use the template to cut hinge mortises as shown in photo 5 (page 88). Align the mortises so the bottom hinges are 3" from the bottom of the doors, and the top hinges are 2" from the top of the doors. Wait to cut the mortises in the doors until after the doors and face frame are glued up so they can be aligned with each other.

Bore holes along the inside face of the side frame stiles for shelf pins. Space them 1" apart, starting about 8" from the bottom of the stiles up to 8" from the top. See the suppliers list at the end of the book for sellers of shelf pins.

Decide what stock you will use for panels on the side frames and doors. A good choice here is ¼" maple or birch veneer plywood. Don't use your good Baltic birch template stock plywood—it's too expensive for this. Whatever you use, you need to have the stock on hand when you cut the grooves for the panels so you can match the width of the groove to the thickness of the panels.

Cut panel grooves on the straight parts with a straight flute bit as shown in photo 6 (page 88).

Make the grooves ¼" deep. Using a bit of lesser diameter than the thickness of the plywood, make two cuts flipping the part between to center the groove. Lower the part over the bit at one of the mortises where it will not hit wood, then push the part into the bit until it goes into the opposite mortise, and lift away. Always keep your fingers away from the area around the bit, even when it is covered with wood. Despite your best efforts, the groove width will vary a bit, so make tests with your plywood to be sure it will fit snug but not too tight. Cut grooves in the curve edge of the top rail using a thin slot cutter as in photo 7 (at bottom).

Bore holes in the wide ends of the door top rails for the floating dowels that will keep the rail aligned to the stile as discussed above. Use a dowel that is wider than the mortise, then trim the dowel on its sides to match, so a flat surface contacts the mortise walls. Don't glue in these dowels. The finished top rail joint will appear as in photo 8 (page 89).

Dry assemble one of the doors, and use it to scribe the shape of the panels for the doors. Add ³/₁₆" around the perimeter of the scribed lines (which are obtained from the inside of the frame), and cut out the panels accordingly. Dry assemble a side frame and measure inside it for the panels. Add ³/₈" to each dimension, and use these numbers to cut out panels.

Glue up all the frames, as shown in photo 9 (page 89). Check each frame for squareness once it is pulled together. You can do so by measuring diagonally across opposite corners and comparing the two measures you get. When they are equal, the frame is square.

Join the front face frames to the side frames with plate joints or dowels. Attach the edge of the side frames to the rear face of the face frame. Align the face of the side frame flush to the edge of the face frame. Glue these together.

Make the back, top and bottom of each cabinet out of ½" or ¾" utility, or "shop" grade plywood. Attach the bottom and top to the side frames and face frame with screw strips that are about ¾" square in profile, and run the whole length of inside of these parts. Align the top screw strips so that the plywood top is flush to the top of the frames. Position the bottom screw strips along the bottom edges of the frames.

Before you put on the back, screw door stop strips onto the inside of the face frames to prevent the doors from swinging inward. Get magnetic door latches at the hardware store, and design the door stops large enough to attach the latches to.

**Photo 5—Cut hinge mortises in the face frame stiles using a template and a router template guide.**

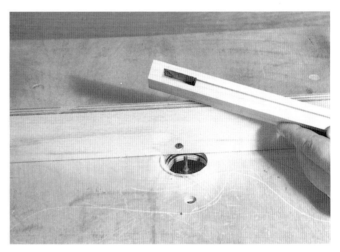

**Photo 6—Rout slots for the panels on the door and side frame parts using a straight flute bit at the router table.**

**Photo 7—Use a bearing-guided slot cutter to make the slots along the curved edge of the door top rails for the door panels.**

Cut the plywood to size. Attach it with screw strips to the plywood top and bottom. Screw the plywood back directly onto the rear edges of the side frames. Place the screws about every 4". This joint will take all the weight of the cabinets, since the plywood backs will be screwed to the wall. So don't skimp on screws!

Don't glue the plywood to the screw strips. Plywood and solid wood expand and contract at different rates with moisture variations, straining a glue joint. Use a lot of screws with properly bored holes.

Size the doors to fit within the face frames by trimming them to size with a hand plane or sizing them on the table saw as you would a piece of plywood. Bevel the meeting edges of the doors so they don't hit each other as they open. When the doors fit in place, mark where the hinge mortises go, then rout mortises into the door edges as you did on the face frames. Install the doors with hinges, magnetic latches and your choice of pulls.

Attach the cabinets to the wall by screwing directly through the plywood back into the wall studs. Secure each cabinet to at least two studs, and use at least four 2" screws in each stud. Place the screws closer to the top of the cabinet.

Apply molding strips along the visible edges of the plywood backs. Stain the cabinets if you like, and finish them with wipe-on oil or polyurethane varnish. Cut out shelves and put them in place with shelf pins.

*Photo 8—Where the wide ends of the door top rails join the stiles, make a second mortise for a dowel. The dowel, which is not glued, keeps the lower portion of the wide rail flush to the stile, while allowing for moisture-related movement.*

*Photo 9—Glue up and clamp together all the frames. Check for squareness by measuring across diagonal corners.*

*Adjustable shelves accommodate your planes, and custom holders on the inside of the doors keep your chisels and other tools.*

**T**his cabinet design takes a different approach to the problem of carcass construction. In the previous chapter, the sides and front of the cabinet were made with frame and panel construction. This cabinet uses solid boards, or plank construction, for all broad surfaces.

Using wide solid lumber like this presents one potential problem—wood movement. All wood expands and contracts across the grain with moisture variations, and the wider the piece of wood the more it will move. This movement wreaks havoc on joinery where the grain of adjoining pieces is at 90°. The wider the piece the greater the movement, and the worse the problem. Frame and panel construction

deals with the problem by allowing wide panels to float within a rigid frame. Plank construction must deal with movement in other ways.

If you were to edge glue together the planks for the back and doors on this cabinet, the total width dimensions on the finished planks would be 36" and 18" respectively. Moisture-related movement across these widths would be enough to break any cross-grain joint on them, such as where the back is secured to the cabinet top and bottom. The solution is to

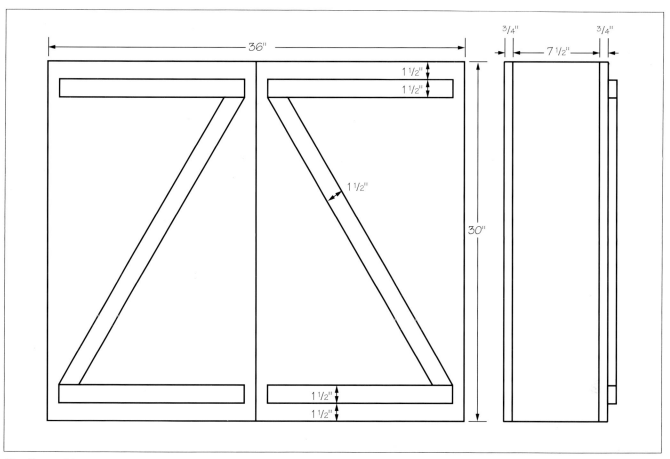

*The diagonal braces on the doors keep the doors from sagging under their own weight. Butt the ends of these braces firmly against the horizontal rails.*

## MATERIALS LIST

| Part | Dimension |
| --- | --- |
| All stock ¾" thick. | |
| A Top and bottom (2) | 7½" × 36" |
| B Sides (2) | 7½" × 30" |
| C Zs (4) | 1½" × 17" |
| D Zs (2) | 1½" × 30" |
| E Shelf supports (4) | 1" × 30" |
| F Shelves (4) | 3" × 34⅜" |

You will also need enough 30"-long pieces to get a total width of 6½ feet for the back and two doors.

*This cabinet uses slab construction for the doors and cabinet back, which is easy to build and gives a rustic look.*

leave individual boards at their existing widths, and not edge glue them together with other boards. This way, each board can expand and contract without affecting other boards, and each board will have less effect on cross-grain joinery.

So that cracks don't appear between individual boards, put an unglued tongue and groove joint

Photo 1—Cut grooves for tongue and groove joints on the router table with a straight flute bit.

Photo 2—Cut tongues on the router table with this setup. Regulate the fit of the tongues in the grooves by the height of router bit.

Photo 3—Join the corners of the cabinet sides with dovetails, preferably through dovetails, using a dovetail jig.

Photo 4—Set a dado blade at an angle in the table saw to cut notches for the shelf supports.

between the boards. This will allow the boards to expand and contract without letting light through. The expansion and contraction of individual boards is enough to break a cross-grain glue joint, but not enough to ruin screws, which have some give to them. This design uses screws to fix the back planks to the carcass top and bottom, as well as to secure the door cross members.

But screws are not adequate to join the four corners of the carcass sides, top and bottom, since the screws would go into end grain where screws are weakest. Therefore, join these corners with dovetails, or with finger joints if you prefer.

Begin by selecting stock for your parts. The top, bottom and sides need to be a certain width, but the planks for the back and doors do not; they can be made of boards of varying widths, just so the total widths are 36" and 18" respectively. This fact helps you save stock since you can use most of your boards

at their existing widths. You just need to reduce the widths enough to straighten them with your straight-edge jig (chapter five).

Account for a 39" width for the back and 20" for each door. The tongue and groove joints will reduce the final width of the back and doors, depending on the number of planks in each. You'll be better off with flat boards for the planks—those not flat will cause problems when you make the tongue and groove joint. Still you can compensate for this, so this is a good project for using some of those not-so-flat boards you set aside. But continue to set those seriously twisted pieces aside; use them in bench or router top laminations.

Rip to width and cut to length planks for the back and doors. Lay them out and mark which edges get tongues and which get grooves. Set up at the router table to cut the tongues and grooves with a ¼" straight flute bit as in photos 1 and 2 (above). Cut grooves

**Photo 5—Make angled cuts on the ends of shelf holders to fit the notches in the supports. These cuts can be made with a handsaw or shaped with a stationary sander.**

possibly break) the router bit. On denser woods you may need to take multiple passes at incremental settings.

Join the top, bottom and side boards using a through dovetail jig as in photo 3 (page 92). You could just as well use half-blind dovetails, but in any event locate the dovetails on the sides and the pins on the top and bottom. Use finger joints if you prefer (chapter six). Glue together the parts and ensure that they are square.

Make adjustable shelf supports with a dado set at the table saw as shown in photo 4 (page 92). Set up the dado at ¾" wide and at a 15° angle in the saw. Cut angled notches into the four supports all at once as shown, placing them 1½" apart and 5" from top and bottom.

Set up to drill holes and set screws with two electric drills—one to bore holes with tapered bits and countersinks, the other with a Phillips bit tip to drive the screws. This second drill ought to be a variable-speed model so you can gently ease the screws down. Use 1¼" screws, and screw the shelf supports onto the insides of the carcass sides. Align the rear supports flush with the rear edges of the sides, and the front edge of the front supports at 3" from the rear edge.

Next screw the back pieces in place placing two screws in the top and bottom of each plank and at every 6" along the sides. Leave ¹⁄₁₆" between each plank after the tongue is engaged in the groove. Rip the final piece to width before screwing it down so that it fits flush to the outer edge.

Similarly screw together the doors, and rip them to width at 18". Chisel mortises in the leading edges of the sides for hinges, but not in the doors themselves. Install magnetic door latches to hold the doors shut. Make small shelf holders as shown in photo 5 (at left) to fit the notches. Cut these out on a band saw or with a small handsaw. Notch the shelf ends to fit around the supports.

Screw the cabinet directly to a wall, but be sure that your screws go into the wall studs; the cabinet is too heavy to be secured to a wall board alone. Fashion holders for your favorite hand tools and screw these inside the doors as shown.

¼" deep in the center of the edges as shown in photo 1. Then reset the location of the router table fence as in photo 2 to cut the tongues, which should be ¼" in height from the finished plank edge. Adjust the thickness of the tongue with the height of the bit above the table. Set the tongue thickness to fit snugly within the groove.

Tongues on warped boards will vary in thickness according to how warped the board is. First cut all the tongues at a setup where flat boards fit fine, then go back and adjust the router for a thinner tongue for the problem boards.

Make the cuts slowly so you don't strain (and

# 25 STATIONARY ROUTER TABLE

A stationary router table offers two advantages over smaller router tables that you can mount on your bench. Aside from the fact that it doesn't take up space on the bench, it gives you storage drawers to keep your bits, routers and related accessories.

The basic carcass construction on this router table is the same as on the cabinet for the workbench in chapter nineteen as well as the grinder cabinet in chapter twenty. However, I'll explore a different means of joinery for the side frames on this piece—dowels rather than open mortise and tenon joints as on the previous pieces. This will make the project a bit easier as you'll see.

Begin by getting out your stock, looking for very straight pieces for the drawer frame components. Since these pieces hold the drawers and guide them as they slide in and out, bowed parts will cause the drawers to bind. However, if the side frame parts are slightly bowed, you will straighten them up when the carcass gets glued up. You should, however, be able to guarantee that all edges are straight with your straightedge jig (chapter five) or a jointer.

Bore the side frame components for ³⁄₈" diameter dowels. Be sure to place the dowel holes away from the panel groove in the bottom and mid rails. Mark dowel hole centers at ⁵⁄₈" and 1¼" from the bottom of the lower rail, and the same distances from the top of the mid rail. On the upper rails, mark the holes at ½" and 1½" from the top. Carefully mark out the parts before boring. Use a doweling jig as in photo 1 (page 95) to bore the holes. Often ³⁄₈" dowel pins purchased in hardware stores are 2" long, so bore just over 1" deep into both the rail ends and post edges.

Next bore the inside faces of the posts for carcass rails as well as the drawer frames. For this you'll need a doweling jig capable of reaching across a 2" width, which some won't do. You can also set up on the drill press for these holes. Center the holes for the drawer frames along the width of the posts, and mark those for the carcass rails at ³⁄₈" from the edge. Set the heights of the holes for the carcass rails so they will be at ½" from the edges of the rails. Bore

*Adjust the distance of this fence from the router bit with the horizontal adjustment bolt located right of center. Then clamp the fence securely in place with the large locking knob left of the adjustment bolt. The outer knobs hold the whole fence assembly in place on the router table.*

these holes at about ⁹⁄₁₆" deep.

Cut out plywood panels for these frames at the given dimensions. Make a groove along the inside edges of the frame parts for the plywood at the table saw. Use a dado, or make multiple cuts with your combination blade, with the depth of cut set at ¼". Stop the cuts along the edges of the posts so that they do not extend above the enclosed lower section of the cabinet. Mark the posts so you can see where to stop the cut as it is made on the table saw, and mark the table saw so you know where the front of the blade

Photo 1—Use a doweling jig to bore holes for dowels that join the rails to the vertical posts, as well as dowels that join the drawer frames to the vertical posts.

Photo 2—Glue together the side frames as shown. Check them for squareness and adjust as necessary.

Photo 3—Join the drawer frames with groove and tenon joints cut at the table saw; glue them as shown. Install drawer guides in the front and rear pieces.

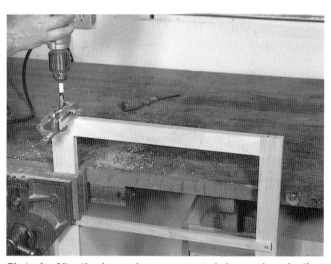

Photo 4—After the drawer frames are out of clamps, bore for the dowels that will join them to the vertical posts in the side frames.

is. Push the part into the cut, and when you see that you have pushed far enough, lift the part off the saw. Keep your fingers away from the blade area!

Before you glue up the side frames, cut a ¼" deep by ¼" wide rabbet along the inside top edge of the mid rails for the plywood table to fit within. Do the same on the inside top edges of the front and rear mid rails, since it's the same setup. Use a dado setup as described in chapter nine. Glue up the side frames as shown in photo 2.

Construct drawer frames exactly like those described in chapter nineteen, using a tenon and groove joint. Fit drawer guides into them as described there and as shown here in photo 3. Note, however, that you only have four mortises to cut for the guides, so unless you already have a router template jig made

for these mortises (as described in chapters thirteen and nineteen), it's easier to cut these by hand with a chisel. Once the drawer frames are assembled, bore them at their corners for the dowels that join them to the posts as shown in photo 4.

Dry clamp together the side frames, but not the drawer frames, with the front and rear rails using ½" long dowels to locate the parts. Cut a ¼" deep by ⅜" wide rabbet along the inside rear edge of the rear bottom rails, mid rails and posts with a router and bearing guided rabbeting bit. This rabbet is for the plywood back. Chisel the corners square.

Glue together the carcass as in photo 5 (page 97). Check for squareness in the front and back, as well as top and bottom. Glue and screw in place twelve corner blocks where the carcass rails join the posts on

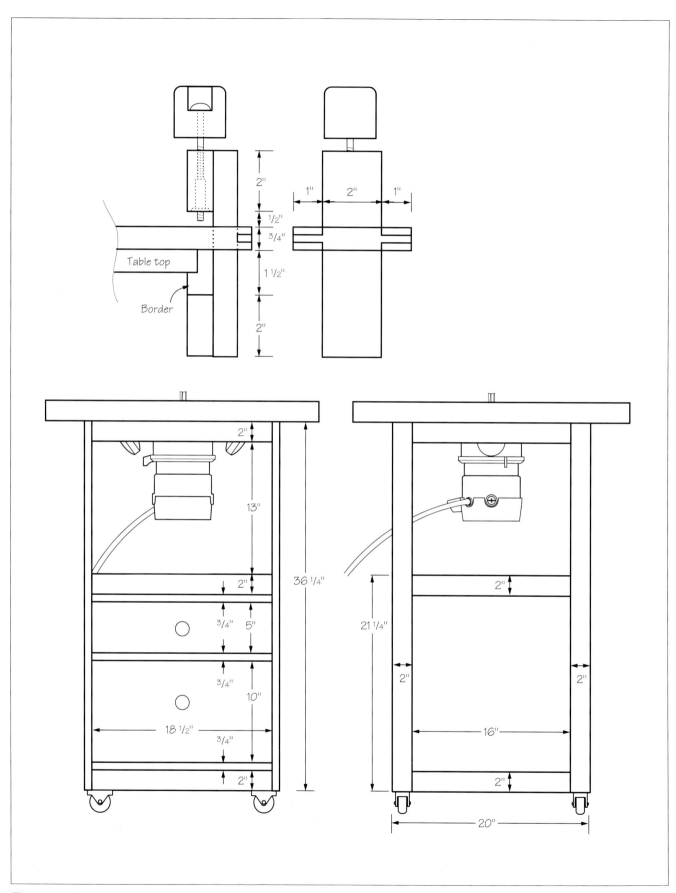

Table top

Border

2"

1/2"

3/4"

1 1/2"

2"

1"

2"

1"

2"

13"

2"

3/4"  5"

3/4"  10"

18 1/2"

3/4"

2"

36 1/4"

21 1/4"

2"

2"

2"

16"

2"

2"

20"

The router table cabinet consists of two side frames with drawer
frames and rails joined between. The fence clamps, shown
above, are specialized wooden C-clamps.

# MATERIALS LIST

| Part | Dimension |
|---|---|
| A  Vertical posts (4) | ¾" × 2" × 36¼" |
| B  Side rails (6) | ¾" × 2" × 16" |
| C  Front and rear rails, and front and rear drawer frame rails (12) | ¾" × 2" × 18½" |
| D  Drawer frame runners (6) | ¾" × 1½" × 17" |
| E  Side plywood (2) | ¼" × 16½" × 17¾" |
| F  Plywood carcass top | ¼" × 19" × 19" |
| G  Drawer front and rear (2) | ½" (or ¾") × 5" × 18⅜" |
| H  Drawer sides (2) | ½" (or ¾") × 5" × 19" |
| I  Drawer front and rear (2) | ½" (or ¾") × 10" × 18⅜" |
| J  Drawer sides (2) | ½" (or ¾") × 10" × 19" |
| K  Plywood drawer bottoms (2) | ¼" × 17⅞" × 18½" |
| L  Drawer guides (2) | ½" × 2" × 18¾" |
| M  Drawer guides (2) | ½" × 1" × 17" |
| N  Particleboard top | ¾" × ¾" × 28" |
| O  Borders (4) | ¾" × 1½" × 30" |
| P  Fence base and fence (2) | ¾" × 5" × 32½" |

Small parts cut to size for fence clamps, hinges, etc. as shown.

Photo 5—Glue together the carcass with a large number of clamps as shown. Check for squareness on the top and bottom as well as on the front and back.

Photo 6—Glue and screw a wood border to the particleboard top. Miter the ends, and cut a shallow rabbet in the border to help align it flush with the top of the table.

the top, bottom and middle.

Make drawers according to the instructions in chapter nineteen, or cut dovetails with your favorite jig, as I did using the jig described in chapter eleven. Note that final dimensions for your drawer parts will depend on your choice of joinery for the drawers. The dimensions given are for drawers with through dovetails, as pictured. Be sure to leave enough clearance for the drawers, both in width and height, so they slide easily, even when humidity increases. Leave 1/16" gap in height for the upper drawer and 1/8" for the lower drawer. Install the drawer guide as shown in chapter nineteen.

I installed fixed rollers on the bottom of the cabinet, because swivel rollers will move as you push work through the table. Fixed rollers will move too, but in one direction only, and their movement can be halted altogether by wedging a scrap of plywood under them before you start using the table.

For the table itself, you can make a laminated top as described in the next chapter, or use ¾" surfaced particleboard as I did. Particleboard is flat and stable making it a good choice here, but it chips and flakes easily so you need to make provisions for this. Melamine is a brand name for a particleboard that is surfaced with thin white laminate. Call a cabinet shop and ask if they'll sell you a piece so you don't have to

buy a whole sheet. A second alternative is to use unsurfaced particleboard and glue laminate to it with contact cement.

Cut out the top and border it with solid wood as in photo 6. Cut a rabbet in the border stock to locate it flush with the table top. Miter the ends, and screw it to the edge. Follow the instructions in chapter twenty-seven for installing your router in the top, with one addition: screw pieces of solid wood on the under side of the top around the hole for the router. Screw the clear plastic plates through the particleboard and into the solid wood.

Attach the top to the rear rail of the cabinet with hinges so you can lift the top to adjust the router depth setting. Again, screw solid wood to the particleboard for the hinges to mount to.

*Photo 7—Cut the slots on the ends of the fence base using your table saw cutoff box as shown.*

*Photo 8—Cut tenons for the lock pieces that hold the side clamps within the slots on the fence base. For safety, make the pieces from long stock as shown. Screw a support fence to your miter gauge to hold the parts as they are cut.*

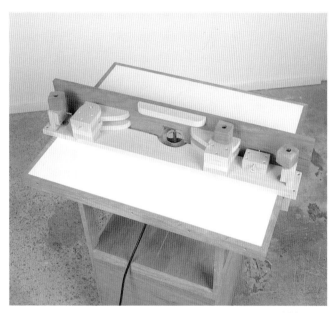

*This router table has drawers for storing your routers and bits. Mounted on rollers, the table conveniently rolls out of the way when not in use.*

The rather elaborate fence on this table has clamps built into it to secure it to the table, as well as an adjustment for fine-tuning the distance of the fence from the bit. All this is accomplished with T-nuts and shop-made knobs that have wooden handles epoxied to carriage bolts. The side clamps fix the base onto the table, then the fence itself pivots on the base. One knob controls the distance of the fence from the base, a second locks the fence in place.

Cut slots on the ends of the base for the side clamps with your cutoff box as shown in photo 7. Cut up to a scribed line as shown, then chop out the waste with a chisel. Next use a tenoning jig to cut open mortises on the remaining ends. Cut the tenons on the lock pieces to fit the open mortises as in photo 8. Since these pieces are short, cut them out of long stock, and then cut them to length after the tenons are done. Attach the lock pieces to the base with screws rather than glue to allow for moisture-related movement in the base.

Assemble the clamps as shown in the drawing. Bore for the T-nuts in the top pieces, then glue and screw them to the long pieces. Place the clamp in the base before gluing and screwing the bottom pieces in place. Epoxy washers to the base beneath the bolt hole so the bolt bears on metal, not wood.

Assemble the fence hinge by stacking the parts together one by one. Place the hinge dowel within the parts as they are stacked to keep it all aligned. The fence clamp is just like the hinge, except that it has a bolt rather than a dowel going through it. Install a T-nut in the base for the fence clamp bolt to secure to. Make $5/8$"-diameter holes in the fence clamp pieces for the bolt.

To adjust the fence, loosen the fence clamp and retract the adjustment bolt. Set the fence clamp in the middle of its travel, which is only about $3/8$". Loosen the side clamps, set the fence to within $1/8$" of where it needs to be, and tighten the side clamps. Tighten the fence clamp and make a test cut. Now adjust the exact location of the fence by loosening the fence clamp and making small adjustments with the fence adjustment screw. Always tighten the fence clamp after making adjustments.

# BENCH TOP ROUTER TABLE

*This small router table easily clamps to the edge of your bench top when in use, and stores under a table or on the wall.*

I f you don't have space in your shop for a stationary router table, or if you want a simpler route to a router table, consider this project. Remember, also, that at times it is handy to have two router tables, and you certainly don't need to build two floor-mounted units. This smaller model is easy to build, store and use, and it will function just as well for most routing purposes as larger models.

On this router table we'll use a different approach to getting a flat table top than that used on the floor model. Rather than find a flat top, you'll make one,

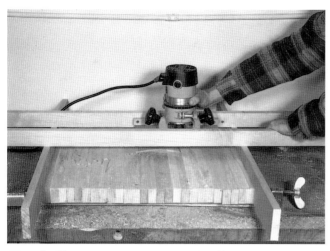

*Photo 1—Flatten the router table top with this router jig, which makes the router travel in straight lines.*

*Photo 2—Screw together the three frames that make up the base.*

using stack laminations of hardwood. This takes more time to make, but in the long run a top like this will hold up better. If you prefer, you can use a particleboard top like that described in the previous chapter.

Begin by getting out all the parts. Note that they are all the same width, but most of the parts for the undercarriage are shorter than those needed for the top. This is useful for making efficient use of your stock. As you look for length combinations that will give you the numerous 20"-long pieces needed for the top, you will often find combinations that give you, say, two 20" and one 18". "Darn," you think, "if only it were two inches longer!" Well don't go buy a board stretcher yet, just use that 18" piece for one of the 16" side rails.

As you get out the pieces, remember that you can use pieces with defects in the stack lamination. There is no need to cut out all the knots and rough edges, so long as each part has one clean edge that you can turn upward for the top. Glue together all the pieces for the top in one gluing operation. Use a lot of glue on the lamination faces, because you are gluing a broad area and much of the glue will be absorbed. Keep hot water and rags close by to deal with the mess.

Keep a close eye on how flat your glue up is. Put your clamps onto a flat surface to begin with so that when you put the pieces on the surface, they will remain flat. As you tighten the clamps on the laminations, some will slide and shift under pressure and because of the slippery glue. Lay a straightedge across the top and correct any discrepancies greater than ⅛". Later you'll rout off that last ⅛", but for now just guarantee that they stay close.

Note that the whole thing can become twisted, like an Oriental fan beginning to open. Conceptually this

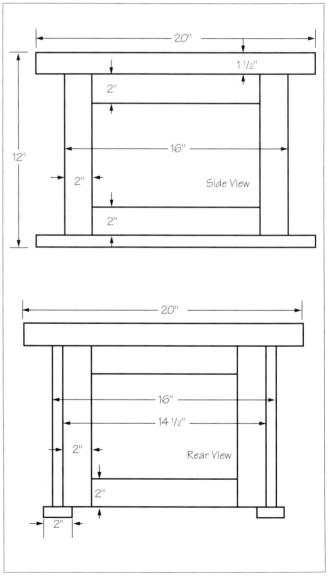

*Make the base of the router table of three frames joined with open mortises and tenons. Screw the frames to each other and to the top.*

*Photo 3—Screw the base to the table top through the top rails as shown, and screw the feet onto the bottom rails.*

## MATERIALS LIST

| Part | | Dimension |
|------|---|-----------|
| A | Laminations for the top (27) | ¾" × 2" × 21" |
| B | Feet (2) | ¾" × 2" × 20" |
| C | Side rails (4) | ¾" × 2" × 16" |
| D | Rear rails (2) | ¾" × 2" × 14½" |
| E | Legs (6) | ¾" × 2" × 11¼" |

is a neat idea but it's devastating for your router table, so watch that the two end laminations stay parallel. To do so use winding sticks, which are two straight sticks of uniform width about 3' long. Place one on one of the end laminations, the other on the other. Stand to the side and align your line of sight along the top edge of both sticks. If the two laminations are not parallel, you will immediately see the discrepancy along the winding sticks. A little out of parallel is not bad at this stage, but use the winding sticks to guarantee that things aren't real bad.

When the lamination is dry, set up to flatten it by clamping two boards with straight edges onto either side of the lamination as in the photo. The top edges of these boards must meet three requirements. They must be straight, they must be parallel, and they must be clamped at close to equal distances from all four corners of the lamination. Use your straightedge jig to meet the first requirement (chapter five). These boards act like winding sticks, so you can sight down them to ensure they are parallel. Measure carefully to align the glue up with the tops of the boards.

The last component in the operation is the router slide jig. This is simply two straight pieces of 1×2

with a plywood router mount in the middle, as shown in photo 1 (page 100). The slide jig rides on top of the straight edge boards clamped to the glue up, and guides the router along a straight path between the two boards. Mount a ½" or greater diameter straight flute bit in the router, and set the depth of cut so that it reaches the lowest area on the lamination surface. Wax the straight edges on the guide boards, turn on the router, and gradually move the router back and forth until you have skimmed over the entire surface of the lamination.

This procedure will produce a flat surface *only* if the guide boards and jig boards are straight and parallel. Another threat to flatness is distortion to the lamination from clamps. Your bar clamps may bow the glue up as pressure is applied. When you cut the surface it will be flat, but when you let off the clamps it springs back and is no longer flat. If your bar clamps bow the lamination, place clamp blocks between the clamp jaws and the wood they contact. Shift the location of these blocks up or down to change the point at which pressure is applied. When pressure is applied at the center of the lamination, it should not bow.

When the top is flat, flip it over and flatten the bottom. This is important so that when you screw the base on, the top won't distort if the screws pull on an uneven surface along the bottom. The top and bottom needn't be exactly parallel, but try to get them close. It's perfect when the thickness is even all the way around.

Make three rectangular frames for the base of the table, using the legs and rails shown on the cutout list. Note that you may wish to increase the height of the six legs according to the height you require beneath the table to fit your particular router. The given dimensions allow 1' clearance, which is adequate for most routers.

Use the table saw tenoning jig to cut open mortise and tenon joints to join the parts of the three frames. Or, cut the rails shorter and use dowels and a doweling jig. Either way, glue up the frames, then clamp the smaller of the three between the inside faces of the two larger ones as in photo 2 (page 100), and screw them together. Use 2" screws and predrill holes for them. Next take this frame and clamp it to the underside of the top as shown in photo 3 (above). Use 2½" screws to secure the frame and top together as shown, again predrilling for the screws.

Lastly, screw the two feet onto the bottom of the two side frames. The feet provide an area for clamping and securing the table to your bench top.

# 27

# MOUNTING A ROUTER IN A TABLE TOP

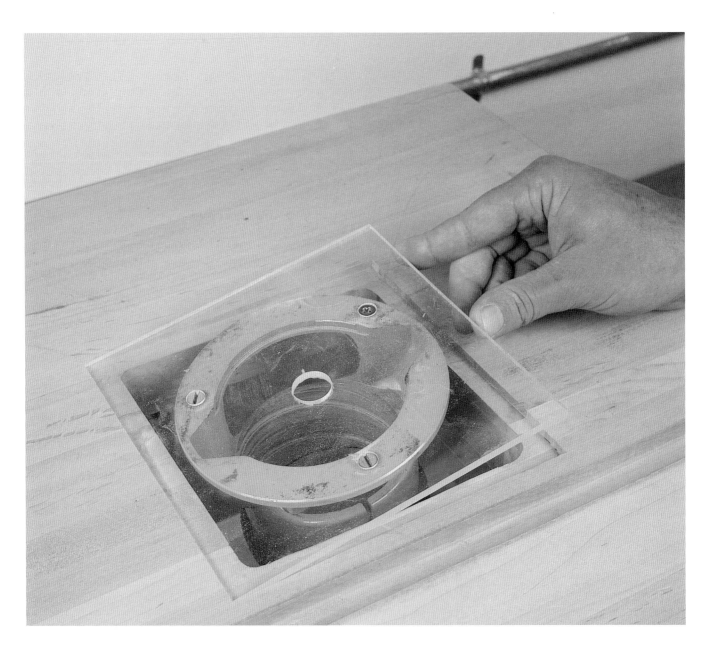

You can make a router table from any bench or table top by installing a router base into the surface. The method for doing so is the same whether you are applying it to an existing bench or building a new router table. An advantage to making a bench top into a router table is the large size of the bench top. It's hard to run long pieces on a small router table, but it's easy

*By mounting your router into its table via a plastic plate, you bring the router base close to the top of the table. Also, you can vary the hole size in the plate by using different plates.*

if the bit protrudes through the middle of a long bench. The disadvantages are that you now have a big hole in your bench, you can't use the router if the bench is being used otherwise, and you can't attach a

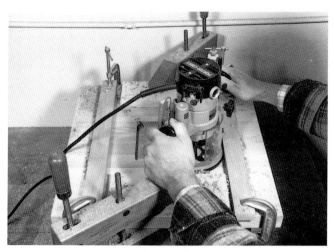

Photo 1—Cut a hole in your router table top using a plunge router and a straight flute bit. Clamp fences around the hole to limit the travel of the router.

Photo 2—Reset the fences ½" behind their first position to cut a rabbet for plastic plates that will hold the router base in place. Carefully adjust the depth of the rabbet to match the thickness of the plastic plates.

fence without cutting more holes in the bench top for C-clamps to stick through. Life is full of compromises.

There are two basic approaches to mounting a router into any table. The first is to simply cut a 1" or 1½" hole in the table, and fix a router base beneath it. This works well for certain operations, but limits the capabilities of your setups for several reasons. First, because the base is below the table top by the thickness of the top itself, the height adjustment of your router is reduced by the thickness of the top. Secondly, you may sometimes want a larger hole for bigger router bits. But, you'll want a smaller hole when you use smaller bits so your parts don't dip into a gaping chasm in the top.

The solution is to mount the router base onto a ¼" clear plastic plate, and fit the plate into the table in a rabbet. This brings the router base as close as possible to the table top, maximizing its height adjustment distance. Plus, you can make two or three plastic plates with different-sized central holes for use with various router bits.

Begin the procedure by cutting a hole in the center of your router table, or in your table top, for the router base to fit in. Make this hole just large enough for the base to fit through, and remember that the handles on most router bases will unscrew to come out of the way. Cut the hole using a plunge router and a ⅜" or larger straight flute bit. Clamp four fences onto the top as in photo 1 for the edge of the plunge router base to butt against. Measure carefully the distance from the bit to the edge of the plunge router base, and mark the fences that distance from where you want the edge of the hole to be.

Make the cut in stages. First set the plunge router

to between ¼" and ⅜", and cut at this setting all around the perimeter of the hole. Also cut inside the outer perimeter another ½" or so to make clearance for the bit as it gets deeper. Then drop the setting another ¼" to ⅜" and cut again. Continue until your plunge setting cuts through the top. But don't cut the central waste chunk free with the router, because it could get caught and thrown by the bit. Cut around ninety percent of its perimeter, then turn off and remove the router, and knock the chunk free with a hammer. Use the router to clean up what's left.

Now move the four fences ½" away from the hole. Check that adjacent fences are all at 90° to each other. Set the plunge router to cut at a depth equal to the thickness of your plastic plate. Make test cuts using a small piece of the plastic to predetermine the depth as in photo 2.

Use a chisel to square up the corners of the rabbet for the plastic. Cut out several squares of plastic that fit with little or no gap between them and the table. Remove the stock plastic base from your router base, and center it on one of the plastic plates. Mark the location of the screw holes that fix the stock plastic base to the router base itself, and mark the center of the base on the plastic plate.

I suggest that you bore these holes on a drill press; plastic cuts differently than wood and can grab a twist bit as it comes through the cut. A Forstner bit is best for boring the large central hole, though a spade bit will also do it. Firmly clamp the plastic in the drill press, and set it on a wood substrate for the bit to go into after the cut is made. Countersink the screw holes so the screw heads will be below the top surface.

S harpening is an essential skill for a wood-worker, because your chisels and plane irons are worthless if they are dull. Sharpening is a less tedious task if you set yourself up so you can easily get out what you need and hop to it. This sharpening station holds your stones at the ready with a base that doubles as a lid for your stone bucket. A raised lip around the edge of the base keeps water or oil from spilling on your bench.

Why store your stones in a bucket? Water stones need to be kept immersed in water; otherwise, when you use them they absorb the water you place on them and the surface quickly dries. The surface must remain wet while you are sharpening to wash away the ground metal. Oil stones don't need to be

*You'll be more inclined to keep your tools sharp if it's easy to set up to sharpen. This station holds what you need all in one place.*

immersed in oil, but the oil on them is messy, and keeping them in a bucket contains the mess.

Get an old plastic five-gallon bucket and cut it off at about 6" above the bottom with a hacksaw. Carefully measure the diameter of the lip at this point. Get a piece of ¾" thick plywood that is 20" square. Use your router radiusing jig (chapter fourteen) and a ¼" straight flute bit to cut a circle groove on the bottom of the plywood, at ¼" deep. See photo 2 (page 105). The groove fits over the top of the bucket so the lid stays in place.

Nail pieces of ⅜" × ¾" stock around the top edge

of the base. Put a layer of waterproof caulking between these pieces and the base itself so water or oil will not leak beneath them or at the corners. Also attach one piece of this stock on the bottom front edge of the base. This lip prevents the base from sliding across the bench top as you push tools across the stones.

Now place two of your stones on the base, and put small holding strips on either end of the stones to hold them in place. Your sharpening station is ready for use.

## How to Sharpen Tools

I use two grades of stones for all my sharpening. I have a 1000-grit stone for smoothing the bevel, and a 6000-grit fine stone for polishing the edge. Both are waterstones, but oil stones will work just fine too.

Establish the proper bevel on your chisels or plane irons with a grinder and medium grit wheel (see chapter twenty). Although 25° is touted as the optimum bevel for these tools, I prefer a greater angle (about 30°) because the edge holds up longer. Once the bevel is established, use honing guides to accurately smooth and polish the bevel on your stones, as shown in the photo above.

After grinding, set the honing guide to hold the bevel on the stone at a few degrees more than the bevel itself, so that the tip of the tool touches the stone and the heel of the bevel does not. Push the tool back and forth on your medium grit stone until about $1/16$" of the tip is smoothed. Go to the fine stone, and move the guide so that it is $1/16$" closer to the tool tip. This increases the angle slightly again, and causes only the tip to be sharpened. There is no need to polish the entire bevel since only the tip needs to be sharp.

The three honing guides shown from left to right are manufactured and sold by Veritas, Leichtung and General. All three will do the job effectively. The General is made of heavy plastic, the others of metal. The Veritas guide has a mechanism that slightly alters the angle at which the tool is held, so you don't need to change the location of the guide between medium and fine stones, as described above. Note that the General honing guide has a wheel that rolls on the table top, not on the stone itself like the others. To use this guide with this sharpening station, you must make the station base 10" longer so the wheel has room to roll on the base surface.

# 29 LARGE TOOLBOX

*Shelves inside the box hold small tools, and larger tools go in the bottom.*

**T**his toolbox is modeled after a basic design that many woodworkers have used over the years, but it makes use of a modern innovation that wasn't available until recently—plywood. Older toolboxes were made of solid planks joined at best with dovetails, and at worst with nails. This may indeed make a very sturdy box, but it is invariably very heavy and can in the long run suffer the problems inherent with wide solid stock—namely, splitting and warping due to moisture variations.

Plywood is light, strong and not noticeably affected by normal moisture variations. Use corner blocks to join plywood pieces at the corners, with screws to fasten the plywood to the blocks. The corner blocks

only need to be thick enough to hold screws well, because the structural integrity of the box comes from the great strength of the plywood rather than the strength of the wooden frames around the plywood. Screws will hold the box together very tightly, and by using a tapered bit with countersink, as well as a variable-speed drill with a Phillips driver bit, installing the screws goes very fast—like riveting together a steel structure.

The best plywood to use for this project is ¼" Baltic birch. This five-layer material is the strongest and most durable plywood commonly available, but unfortunately it is also one of the most expensive. Other less expensive alternatives are available. Find out what's on the shelf at your local supplier. Beware of very cheap materials like CDX construction plywood, which may not take screws very well. If you use a plywood thicker than $\frac{1}{4}$", you will need to adjust some of the dimensions of parts on the project, since the thickness of plywood is one element of some dimension totals.

Start by making the four frames that function as the corner blocks for joining the plywood plates. There are two duplicate frames that go on either end of the box, and one frame each for the top and the bottom. The latter two are not duplicates; the bottom is a bit smaller than the top.

Join the frames with open mortise and tenon joints at the corners, and through joints for the middle members. Begin with the through mortises for the middle members, then set up on the table saw with a tenoning jig as shown in chapters three and seven to make tenons to fit those mortises. Cut all the tenons at the same time, then use the tenoning jig to cut the open mortises on the ends of parts to match the tenons.

If you have a chisel mortiser for your drill press, now is a good time to put it to use for the through mortises that join middle members on all frames. But if you don't have a chisel mortiser, then simply bore a series of holes at each mortise location and then clear out the waste with a chisel. First carefully measure along the lengths of the parts and mark the ends of each mortise. Use a $\frac{5}{16}$" bit, and carefully center the cut along the $\frac{3}{4}$" width of the parts. If you don't have a drill press, this can be just as easily done with a doweling jig. Cut as many holes between your marks as you can fit.

Once the holes are cut, place the piece in a vise and align a broad chisel along the edges of the holes as in photo 1 (page 109). Tap with a mallet to cut a line here. This line establishes the width of the mortise. Make a similar cut along the ends of the mortise with a smaller chisel, then clear out the waste at the top. This should bring you to a depth of $\frac{3}{16}$" or so. Repeat the procedure to deepen the mortise, but don't cut all the way through. Once you are about halfway through, flip the part and repeat the procedure from the other side. If you do bang all the way through from one side, you risk splitting out the mortise edges on the other side.

Be careful not to widen the mortises any more than the width of the holes, so that all the mortises come out to $\frac{5}{16}$" wide. Once the mortises are finished, set up the tenoning jig to cut tenons that match the

*This traditional toolbox makes good use of a modern innovation—plywood.*

mortises. When making your first tenon, cut it thicker than you need at first, and then carefully fine-tune the adjustments on the jig to gradually reduce the tenon thickness to match the mortise. Because you are flipping the part for each pass, adjustments to the jig or saw are doubled since the additional amount of cut comes off two sides. Make small adjustments to slowly bring the tenons to size.

Once the tenons for the through mortises are complete, cut out the other tenons for the open mortises at the same setting. Once these are cut, make the open mortises to match these tenons. Make the open mortises on the tenoning jig by using a reverse procedure to the tenoning: First make the mortises too small, and gradually adjust the jig to enlarge the mortises until they fit the tenons. Through mortises are the most difficult to adjust for thickness, whereas the tenons and open mortises are far easier to adjust by using the jig. That's why you should make the through mortises first—it's easier to make the tenons and open mortises match the through mortises rather than vice versa.

Before the side frames can be assembled, you must cut the wide tenon on the central handle plate into two tenons to fit the two mortises that were cut here. You need two mortises and tenons here because a single wide mortise would be very weak. Mark the wide tenon and make two hand saw cuts to establish the tenon shoulders. Then chisel out the waste.

Your parts should now appear as in photo 2 (page 109). Test fit each frame to be sure that all the joints go together well, then glue and clamp together the joints with C-clamps and clamp blocks. The clamp pressure needn't be excessive but should be enough to

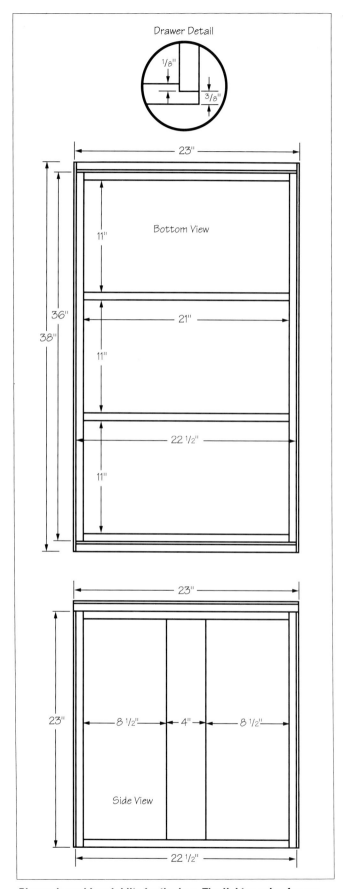

**Drawer Detail**

1/8"
3/8"

23"

Bottom View

11"
21"
11"
22 1/2"
11"

36"
38"

23"

23"

8 1/2"  4"  8 1/2"

22 1/2"

Side View

**Plywood provides rigidity for the box. The light wooden frames around the perimeter are for screwing the plywood together and holding hardware.**

## MATERIALS LIST

| Part | | Dimension |
|---|---|---|
| **¼" Plywood** | | |
| A | Front, back, and top (3) | 23" × 38" |
| B | Bottom | 22½" × 36" |
| C | Sides (2) | 22½" × 23" |
| D | Shelves (3) | 22⅜" × 18" |
| **¾" × ¾" Hardwood** | | |
| E | Sides and bottom frame rails (8) | 22½" |
| F | Side frame posts and top frame rails (8) | 23" |
| G | Bottom frame rails (2) | |
| H | Inside shelf runners (8) | 36" |
| I | Top frame rails (2) | 38" |
| **Other hardwood** | | |
| J | Inside top rails (2) | ¾" × 2" × 36" |
| K | Inside top rails (2) | ¾" × 2" × 21" |
| L | Side handle plates (2) | ¾" × 4" × 23" |
| **Shelves- ½" stock** | | |
| | (2) | 1½" × 18" |
| | (2) | 1½" × 21⅞" |
| | (2) | 1⅞" × 18" |
| | (2) | 1⅞" × 21⅞" |
| | (2) | 3⅝" × 18" |
| | (2) | 3⅝" × 21⅞" |

ensure that all the joints close. Check to be certain that the frames are square.

The next step is to cut out the plywood plates. For this you'll need two 4'×8' sheets of ¼" plywood, or one 4'×8' sheet and one 5'×5' sheet. Some hardwood plywood comes in 5'×5' sheets, and you can save some money this way. But you may want to get two large sheets anyway because the extra wood will come in handy for making jigs and other projects in this book.

When you try to make the first cut on a large sheet of plywood at the table saw, you will find the sheet is so large that it is unwieldy. Get a second person to help. Always be sure that the edge of the plywood that rides against the saw fence is held firmly against the fence. Apply pressure at a 45° angle toward the fence and forward, with your hands between the blade and the fence. If the plywood comes away from the fence and gets above the blade, the blade can grab it and throw the whole sheet—so be careful. See chapter fifteen for another method of making the first cuts on a sheet with the table saw. Either way, always cut

Photo 1—Cut mortises in the side frame rails for the side handle plate tenons by first boring holes and then chiseling out the waste.

Photo 2—The side frames will appear like this when the joinery is complete. Glue the joints together, and place C-clamps on them to pull the mortises onto the tenons.

oversize $\frac{1}{4}$" or so on the first few cuts and then trim the pieces to size later.

With the plywood cut out, make and assemble the shelves. Cut the shelf sides out of $\frac{1}{2}$" stock, and rabbet the ends of the shorter sides with $\frac{1}{4}$"×$\frac{1}{2}$" rabbets. You can cut the rabbets on the table saw using the miter gauge and dado set as in chapter nine, or with a tenoning jig. Glue and screw (or nail) the shelf corners together, then attach the plywood bottom to each in the same way.

The shelves ride on runners that are fixed to the front and rear plywood plates. Carefully measure to locate these runners, and screw them on from the outside of the piece. To hold the runners secure on the

inside of the plywood while you screw from the outside, clamp the runners in place on the ends with thumbscrews or large C-clamps as in photo 3 (page 110).

A note on installing screws—because you have a lot to deal with on this project, it pays to set yourself up to do this efficiently. If you don't yet have a set of tapered bits with adjustable countersinks, now is a good time to get some. For spinning the screws down, a variable-speed drill with a screw driver tip is fast and easy, and saves your hands and forearms the real labor of turning all those screws. I have one inexpensive single-speed drill that I use to drill holes, and one expensive variable-speed drill for setting screws. These days there are less expensive variable-speed drills available. Use Phillips screws only on a project like this because it is a lot easier to keep the bit in the screw head.

Begin assembling the box by screwing the side, bottom and top plywood plates to their frames with ³⁄₄" screws. You may find that the frames are not perfectly square and don't line up with the edges of the plywood, but because the frames are relatively light, you'll find that you can rack them slightly so that all the edges do line up. Place screws every 4" to 6" or so. Next attach the sides to the bottom. The screws here need to be 1½" long, because they go through the side frame and plywood and anchor into the bottom frame. Once this is done the rear plywood plate can be screwed to the rear of the side and bottom frames. Be sure the runners for the shelves are toward the top of the box.

Place the box on its back, and put the shelves in the box alongside their runners. Now lower the front into position, working the fronts of the shelves between the runners on the inside of the front as in photo 4. Screw down the front.

Lift the box onto its bottom and check to see that the shelves slide freely. Now attach the top inside rails along the inner lip of the box top with screws from the outside. Fasten four support angle irons at each corner as in photo 5. I used four hinges to secure the top to the back, and found some standard box handles to attach to the side handle plates. Don't skimp on the casters; they will carry a fair amount of weight and cheap ones will break. If you want to lock your box, or just secure it shut, install a latch for a padlock or a wooden wedge.

Carpenters that took their toolboxes on the job usually built fixtures on the inside of the top to hold their saws. Custom design a set of holders to fit your saws if you want to add this touch.

Rub a candle on the runners for the shelves to keep them moving freely. A coat or two of satin polyurethane on the outside will protect the box from spills, but I left the inside unfinished so the fresh smell of birch plywood would not go away. Years later, it's still there.

**Photo 3**—Attach the shelf runners to the front and rear plates with screws from the outside of the plates. Hold the runners in place with clamps, as shown, while the screws are set.

**Photo 4**—The shelves must be in place within the box when the front plate is put in position and screwed down. As you lower the front plate, be sure that the shelves engage between the correct runners.

**Photo 5**—Install angle irons on the top inside corners to stiffen the box.

# 30 MAKING HANDSCREWS

**You can easily make handscrews for half the cost of ready-made clamps using kits that contain the hardware. You make the wooden jaws.**

I t's often said that you can't have too many clamps, but buying as many as you want can break the bank. You can reduce the cost significantly by making your own, and handscrews are a prime candidate for this. Kits for making handscrews are readily available with threaded rods and handles you need (see the suppliers list). All you supply is the lumber and sweat.

You can conceivably make all the components for your handscrews. However, you would need to buy both right- and left-handed thread taps and dies—which are not inexpensive—and you would need a lathe for turning the handles. The kits, however, provide all this for you, at a total cost of about half of what new handscrews cost.

Get your handscrew kits before you proceed with the project. The kits will contain instructions on how to proceed, as well as specifications for the sizes of the wooden jaws and hole sizes to be bored in the jaws. In each jaw you will need to bore holes for both the rod pins and for the rods themselves. For the rod pins you can use a spade bit, but for the rod clearance holes, which are at an angle, get a Forstner bit. These bits are expensive, but their design allows them to enter the wood at odd angles without deflecting, which is important here.

Photo 1—Smooth the angled cut on the jaw ends with a hand plane or belt sander.

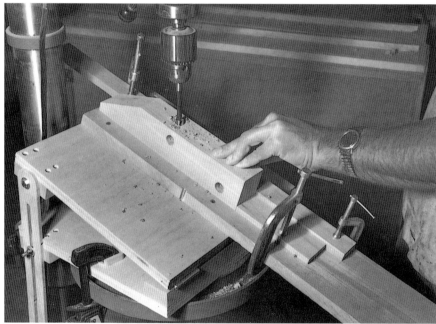

Photo 2—Use your tilt table for the drill press to cut angled holes for the threaded rods to move within.

If you can, use a hard, dense wood, like maple or oak, for the jaws since these woods hold up better over time. But this is a good project for using up short pieces of thick scrap you have accumulated around the shop. If you have a lot of short ¾"-thick pieces available, consider laminating them together to get the thickness you need. The kit instructions will specify certain dimensions for your pieces; however, if your stock is close but not quite the right width or thickness, go ahead and use it. What is important is that you align the holes properly, not that the jaws be at specific dimensions.

Bring your stock to thickness, width and length on the table saw. Mark the angle cut on the front of the jaw as specified in the kit instructions. You can cut this angle on the table saw with a taper jig as in chapter three, but only if the jig is capable of cutting this large an angle. The manufactured taper jigs I have seen are not capable of this, but you can make your own with the necessary capacity. Alternative methods for cutting out the angle are using a band saw or a handsaw. Clean up the surface with a belt sander or hand plane, as in photo 1.

Bore the pin holes in the sides of the jaws on the drill press. It is important that you bore these holes square to the outer surface so that the jaws will seat properly. The kit instructions will tell you exactly where to place them. To prevent tearout as the bit breaks through the bottom side, place a loose piece of scrap beneath the jaws. Move this piece an inch to the side after each cut so that on each successive hole the bit breaks into fresh wood, not into a hole from the previous cut.

Set up your tilt table on the drill press as in photo 2 (page 112). See chapter fifteen for instructions on how to build the tilt table. Refer to the kit instructions to determine what angle you set the table at. The exact angle is not critical. What is important is that the threaded rods have room to move as they pivot on the pins.

You will have to complete numerous small setups for each of these cuts. To locate each one, place the jaw adjacent to the Forstner bit, not below it, and lower the bit until it is close to the pin hole. Move the jaw up or down the slope of the tilt fence until the Forstner bit is centered in the pin hole. Mark the location of the bottom of the jaw on the tilt table, and clamp a stop block here, as in photo 2. Center the jaw under the bit with a fence clamped to the tilt table as shown, and proceed with the cut.

Clean out the waste between the angled holes with a chisel as in photo 3. Use a broad chisel to start the cuts and establish the edges of the slots. Then use a narrower chisel on the inside to clean out the waste where the slots taper down.

The kit will have specific instructions for assembling the threaded rods onto the jaws with the pins. Follow these carefully, because the pins must be spaced properly on the rods for the jaws to close all the way. Check that the jaws will close as in photo 4.

Thread the handles onto the threaded rods, and bore holes for the small shear pins that secure the handles to the rods. Place the handle in a vise as shown in photo 4, and bore through the handle and threaded rod simultaneously. Hammer the pins in place as shown. Coat your new handscrews with wipe-on oil so they won't take on or lose moisture too quickly and crack.

*Photo 3—Chisel the waste out from between the angled holes.*

*Photo 4—The clamp instructions tell you to locate the shear pins through the metal ferrules on the end of the handles. I prefer to place them along the wider body of the handle, because the ferrules on my handles are very thin and loose.*

# 31 SMALL TOOL CHEST

**O**ver the years I've accumulated a lot of small tools like drill bits, calipers and small screw drivers, which are hard to keep track of. All of the small drawers on this little tool chest are perfect for holding these kinds of tools. Build this box using the finger joint (or "box joint") setup described in chapter six, and a mortising chisel on the drill press (chapter sixteen). The project requires ⅜"-thick stock, which is easy to get if you have a planer. If you don't have a planer, there is an alternative—resawing, which is covered below.

Begin by picking your stock. There is a lot of wood

*Exposed finger joints on this box make it very attractive. Make two of them, and use the second for jewelry.*

that goes into this little box because of all the dividers and drawers. There is no need to use good hardwood on the internal drawer parts since they won't be seen, so consider using a less expensive wood like alder or even a softwood like pine. For the drawer fronts I used figured walnut I'd been saving for just such a project. For the box and dividers, I used oak. Note that the alder I used for the drawer sides contrasts highly with the walnut fronts, showing off the joinery.

Pick straight parts for this project. Twisted parts

Use this box in the shop to store all those little gadgets that get lost in larger drawers.

Photo 1—Resaw thick stock by cutting on edge at the table saw using a thin kerf blade.

Photo 2—When you resaw as in photo 1, you may not be able to completely separate some wide boards because your table saw blade goes only so high. Cut the last bit with a rip saw as shown, or on the band saw.

Photo 3—Cut a groove for the drawer bottoms on the table saw with your combination blade raised to ⅛" above the table.

will give you a lot of headaches when you resaw. But note that if you take a long board that has a slight but even bow in it, and cut that into short parts, the parts will be very close to being straight. Note also that this is a good project for using up a lot of short stock you've accumulated from other projects.

Plane your stock to thickness if you have a planer. If you don't, you can resaw the stock to thickness on a band saw (chapter fifteen). If you have neither a band saw nor a planer, you can resaw on the table saw using the following procedure.

Rip the parts to be resawn to ⅛" over width. Set your table saw fence to just over ⅜" from the blade, about ¹³⁄₃₂". If you have a thin kerf saw blade, put it on your saw, otherwise use a rip blade or a combination blade. Raise the blade to ¾" above the table. Make cuts on the edges of the pieces as in photo 1 (top right). When all these cuts have been made, raise the blade to 1½", and cut again. This will cut free the parts for the smaller drawers, but the larger drawers, outer box parts and dividers will not yet be separated. Continue raising the blade in ¾" increments until the parts are cut free or you reach the maximum height of the blade.

A word of caution: Always keep your fingers above the height of the blade when passing over the blade. Don't put your fingers along side the work where the blade is, because the thin stock could shatter, exposing the blade.

Some of your parts will not be separated,

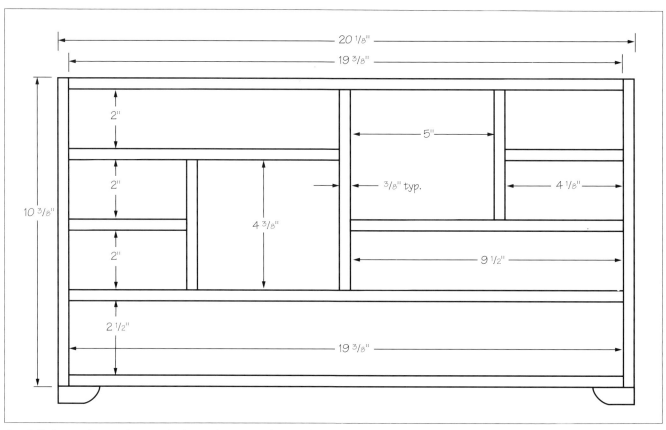

*Carefully locate the mortises for the internal shelf dividers so that the shelves will fit well between.*

depending on the blade's diameter and the width of the parts. Cut the remaining inch or so between the two thin parts with a handsaw as in photo 2 (page 115). A band saw will also quickly separate the two.

Whether you used a band saw, table saw or combination of the two to resaw your parts, one face of each will be somewhat rough and uneven. Smooth and flatten the face with a belt sander or a hand plane. It is difficult to get the thickness of the parts consistent this way, but the parts do not need to be exactly $3/8$" all over for the finger joints and tenons to work well. Get the pieces as close as you can, and use a straightedge placed at 90° to the grain to see if the middle is thicker or thinner than the sides.

When you are satisfied with the thicknesses, rip them to final width and cut them to length. Set up to cut the finger joints on the outer box parts and all drawers, as described in chapter six. Use the width of your carbide combination blade as the width for the fingers or, if you choose, set up with a dado at $1/4$" wide or more.

Take extra care when cutting the finger joints on the wide parts for the two tall drawers and the outer box parts. There are many fingers on each of these joints, and if you inadvertently push one during the progression of cuts that make up the joint, it may

become misaligned. Test the joint as you go to be sure the fingers and slots stay properly aligned.

Begin the bottom of each drawer front with a slot, and begin the bottom of each drawer side with a finger. Once you have cut all the finger joints, cut a groove along the bottom inside of each drawer part for the drawer bottom. Make this groove with your combination blade at the table saw as in photo 3 (page 115). Align this groove so it falls into the lowest slot on the drawer sides and does not cut into the fingers above or below. Conversely, the groove on the drawer fronts should cut only in the lowest finger. This hides the drawer bottom groove from view. The groove will be visible on the drawer sides as a cut in the end of the lowest finger on the drawer front, but this is not visible when the drawer is closed. Make the groove $1/8$" deep.

Cut out $1/4$" plywood pieces for the drawer bottoms. Next set your table saw rip fence at a distance from the blade equal to the groove width you cut on the drawer parts, and raise the blade to just over $1/8$". Place the upper face of each drawer bottom against the rip fence, and push through the blade once on all four sides. This makes a tongue around the drawer bottom that fits the thin groove. Glue together the drawers and clamp them up as in photo 4 (page 117).

## MATERIALS LIST

| Part | | Dimension |
|---|---|---|

All stock is ⅜" thick, except the drawer bottoms and back, which is ¼".

Top, bottom, sides and internal dividers

| | | |
|---|---|---|
| A | Top and bottom (2) | 7" × 20⅛" |
| B | Sides (2) | 7" × 10⅜" |
| C | Shelf | 6¾" × 20⅛" |
| D | Shelves (2) | 6¾" × 10¼" |
| E | Vertical | 6¾" × 7½" |
| F | Vertical (2) | 6¾" × 5⅛" |
| G | Shelves (2) | 6¾" × 4⅞" |

Drawer faces (attractive hardwood)

| | |
|---|---|
| (1) | 2½" × 19⅜" |
| (2) | 2" × 9½" |
| (4) | 2" × 4⅛" |
| (2) | 4⅜" × 5" |

Drawer sides and backs (any wood)

| | |
|---|---|
| (1) | 2½" × 19⅜" |
| (2) | 2" × 9½" |
| (4) | 2" × 4⅛" |
| (2) | 4⅜" × 5" |
| (2) | 2½" × 6⅜" |
| (12) | 2" × 6⅜" |
| (4) | 4⅜" × 6⅜" |

Drawer Bottoms (¼" plywood)

| | |
|---|---|
| (1) | 18⅞" × 5⅞" |
| (2) | 9" × 5⅞" |
| (2) | 4½" × 5⅞" |
| (4) | 3⅝" × 5⅞" |

Back

| | |
|---|---|
| (1) | ¼" × 9⅝" × 19⅜" |

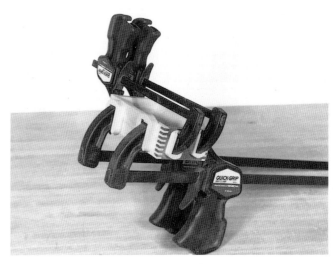

*Photo 4—Glue together the drawers with bar clamps, but apply a minimum of pressure so you don't distort the parts.*

*Photo 5—Cut square mortises for the shelf tenons with a chisel mortiser at the drill press. Carefully align the holes with fences.*

*Photo 6—Use the mortises to mark out the tenons that will fit them. Lay the mortised pieces directly on the edges that will get the tenons, and mark through the mortises as shown.*

Don't put glue on the drawer bottoms or their grooves. Be sure the drawers stay square, and don't clamp so hard that you flex the sides inward.

Mark the outer box sides and internal dividers for the mortises that join the dividers and the sides. Take extra care as you mark these so the mortises will be accurately located. The drawers will not fit properly if the spaces for them are too small.

Set up on the drill press with a mortising attachment to cut three mortises along each joint as shown in photo 5. Place a fence on the drill press to locate the distance of the mortises from the end of the part. Use a stop block on the fence as shown to locate the distance from the edge of the part for the mortises. You will have many duplicate setups between similar parts, so take advantage of this fact and cut as many like holes on each setup as you can.

Photo 7—Cut the waste between the tenons with a dado blade at the table saw. For safety, screw a wide fence to the miter gauge and use this as a support while making the cuts.

Photo 8—Fit together the internal parts. Then put the outer sides on, and fit the top and bottom on.

Locate mortises at $\frac{1}{2}$" from the edges of parts, and at the center. Note that the internal parts are not as wide as the outer parts, which leaves space for the plywood back that fits within the outer sides and against the back of the internal parts.

Use the mortises to mark the sides of the tenons on the ends of the internal parts, as in photo 6 (page 117). Carefully mark each part so you know which side is toward the front of the box, and which face is up, as well as whether the part is located on the right or left of the box.

Screw a 4"-tall fence to your miter gauge, as in photo 7. Set up a $\frac{1}{2}$"-wide dado in the saw, and raise it to $\frac{3}{8}$". Place the internal parts on end on the miter gauge fence as shown, and cut away the waste between tenons, carefully noting the markings on each tenon. Test fit each part end to its corresponding mortises, and make adjustments in the tenon widths until they fit.

Fit all the internal parts together, and fit them to the external sides as shown in photo 8. You don't need to glue the mortises and tenons together, because they will be locked in by the external parts. Test the fit of the top and bottom pieces; then glue and clamp them in place. Using the same procedure for gluing up drawers, check for squareness and don't clamp so hard that the sides flex.

Belt sand the sides of the drawers and outside of the cabinet to smooth the joints. Glue small stop tabs onto the back of the internal parts to limit the travel of the drawers. Screw large roundhead screws onto the drawer fronts for pulls. Cut out a piece of $\frac{1}{4}$" plywood to fit inside the outer edges of the box sides, and nail it in place in the back. Finish sand and cover with wipe-on oil or the finish of your choice.

# 32 HEIGHT HOLDER

O ccasionally you'll need your vice to hold large work, such as a door or long board. Such work needs to be supported on the far end. This simple, adjustable design for a height holder lets you support that far end at the necessary height.

All the pieces for this project can be made from 3/4"×2" stock, except the ratchet, which should be about 3" wide. Make the center bar 30", and cut the others to reasonable size.

Cut ratchet slots into the center bar as explained for shelf supports in chapter twenty-four. Space the slots about 2" apart, and make them about 5/16" deep. Glue and screw the four feet around the base of the center bar.

The ratchet mechanism has five parts: the ratchet, the dowel, two side pieces, and a center piece opposite the ratchet. Position the center piece just far enough away from the ratchet so the whole mechanism can slide up and down when the ratchet is up. See the photo (bottom left), but close enough that the ratchet seats firmly in the ratchet slots when weight is applied to it from above as in the photo (bottom right). Make this adjustment with a clamp as shown, then screw the side pieces to the center piece securely.

*When you put long boards or doors in a vise, support them at the far end with this holder.*

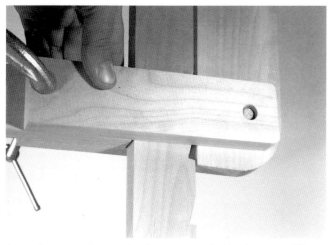

*Leave just enough room for the center and side pieces to slide over the ratchet.*

*When pressure is applied, the center piece becomes locked in the ratchet.*

# 33 MAKING BAR CLAMPS

**B**ar clamps are expensive, but you can save money by buying the screws (see suppliers list) and making your own. These clamps will not apply as much pressure as steel clamps, but they will work well in most applications in a hobbyist's shop.

Use hardwood for these clamps, such as short cut-off pieces from other projects. Use ¼" Baltic birch plywood for the side plates, because it is very strong and you'll need that strength here.

Cut ratchets in the bars with a dado set at an angle in the table saw (see photo 1, page 121). Cut the ratchets about ½" deep, then use a chisel to complete the slot as shown in the drawing. Glue together the fixed heads, minus the bars, then bore holes for the

*Make use of scrap lumber to assemble your own bar clamps for moderate-duty clamping jobs.*

screws to fit as in photo 2 (page 121). You'll need two holes—one for the threaded shaft and one of greater diameter for the threaded fitting that the shaft threads into. Measure shaft and fitting for the proper diameters. The fitting has small wings that secure it in its hole. Cut slots for these in the hole with a chisel.

Make the moving head from four pieces as shown in the drawing. Cut grooves in the two outer pieces at the table saw to fit the outer tabs of the metal pressure fitting, which goes on the end of the screw. Slide the fitting into the grooves as shown in photo 3 (page 121).

Photo 1—Cut angled notches in the bar of your bar clamp with a dado set at the table saw. Use your miter gauge to support the cut.

Photo 2—Setup at the drill press to bore holes in the fixed head for the screw mechanism. Two diameters are required, one for the screw and one for its fitting.

The adjustable head (which fits into the ratchet slots) must do two jobs: hold securely under pressure, and be moveable to another ratchet slot. Carefully align the parts as shown in the drawing so that the part that fits into the ratchet slot seats securely under pressure. Note the critical distance between this piece and the pressure head. This must be larger than the width of the bar so that the adjustable head can slide along the bar when not in a ratchet. Use plenty of glue for assembling all three heads and for attaching the fixed head to the bar.

Photo 3—The metal pressure fitting must be set in grooves in the moving head so the head is retracted as the screw is reversed.

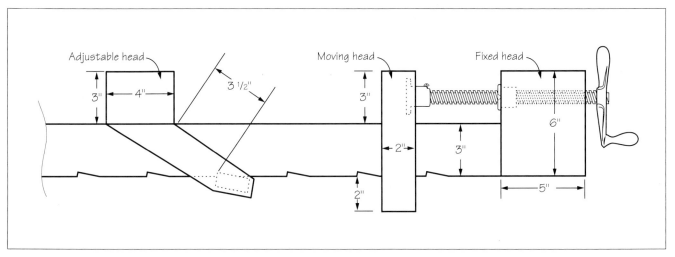

Note that for the adjustable head to move along the bar, there must be adequate distance between the head above and the small block below that fits in the bar notches.

# CLAMP STORAGE

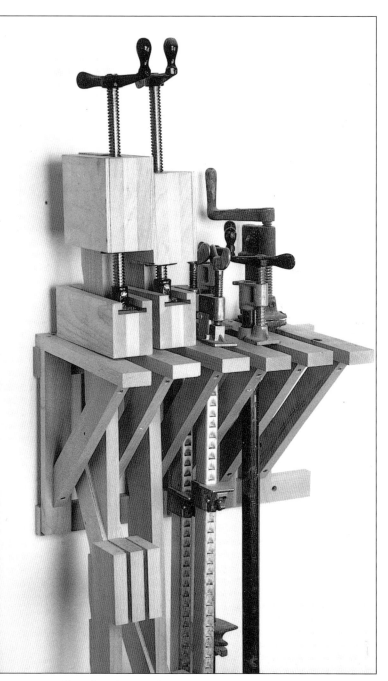

*These bar clamp racks adjust for any width of bar that your clamps might have.*

**B**uild these storage fixtures to get your clamps up on the wall and out of the way when not in use.

### Bar Clamps

The idea here is to set up horizontal plates with slots that can store your bar clamps. The bars on different bar clamps come in varying widths, so it's best to have different slot widths on the storage fixture to accommodate your different clamps. This design lets you make whatever slot widths you need for the clamps you have.

The two main components to this fixture are the triangle plate assemblies and the wall plates. Cut the 45° angles for the triangle support rails on the table saw with your miter gauge. Screw together the triangle plate assemblies as shown in the drawing. Be sure the top and rear plates are at 90° to each other.

Screw the upper wall plate directly to studs in the wall. The lower plate is a spacer and takes no weight, so it can be attached to the wall board or paneling.

Screw the triangle plate assemblies to the upper wall plate as shown in the drawing, and space them as you need to for your clamps.

### Handscrews

You can get the steel pipe fittings for this handscrew storage fixture at any hardware store with plumbing supplies. Most will have 1' sections of threaded pipe on hand, or you can have them made in any length you need. Screw the top fitting to a joist in the ceiling—not to the ceiling wall board, which isn't strong enough for the weight.

### Small Bar Clamps

Again you want to secure this to the wall studs. Angle the dowels upward slightly so the clamps will stay on nicely. Set up on the drill press with your tilt table as described in chapter fifteen, or do as I did, and just eyeball the angle using a hand drill. Secure the base piece in a clamp when you do so.

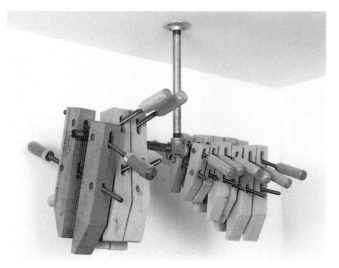

*Commonly available pipe and connectors make this simple handscrew storage device.*

*Store small bar clamps on a peg rack. Angle the pegs upward slightly.*

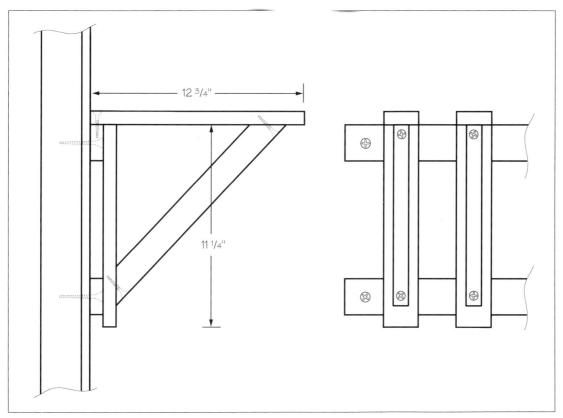

12 ³/₄"

11 ¹/₄"

*Assemble triangular supports as shown, and screw these to plates that are screwed to the wall studs.*

# 35 FOLDING ASSEMBLY TABLE

This design uses the old folding-card table idea, where each of the four legs folds along one side of the table top. Each leg has its own separate hinge that it pivots on. To lock the legs in their open position, all you do is tighten four wing nuts.

Begin the project with a piece of ¾"-thick plywood that measures 4' square. Cut out four 40" rails from 2×4s, and make lap joints at their corners using a dado blade on the table saw as in chapter nine. Clamp these four rails to the plywood using handscrews. Put glue on the lap joints, and screw the rails to the plywood from the top of the table. Countersink the screw heads so they are below the surface.

Cut out four ¾"-thick plywood spacers at 3½"×20". Screw them to the rails as shown. These spacers provide room for the support triangles. Next cut out the support triangles from ½" or ¾" plywood. Cut the angle on them at the band saw or with a saber saw. Attach the folding triangles to the spacers with small cabinet

hinges. Don't yet bore the holes for the bolts and wing nuts that attach the legs to the triangles.

Cut out the four legs from 2×4s, and bore holes for the triangle bolts through the legs 14" from the top. Install ⅜"×5" carriage bolts in each of the holes. Attach the legs to the spacers (as shown in the drawing) with 3½" interior door hinges. Note that the legs are inset from the corners by 1½". This prevents the screws for the leg hinges from going into the lap joint, where they would not be as strong. Use 2" screws that will go through the spacer and into the rail beneath.

Now lift a leg into its open position, and raise its triangle support until it hits the end of the carriage bolt. Mark the spot, and bore a hole there for the bolt. Put on a washer and a wing nut, and proceed to the next leg.

A nice finishing touch is a banding around the edges of the plywood to hide it and protect it from chipping. Glue and screw it in place, and you're ready to use the table.

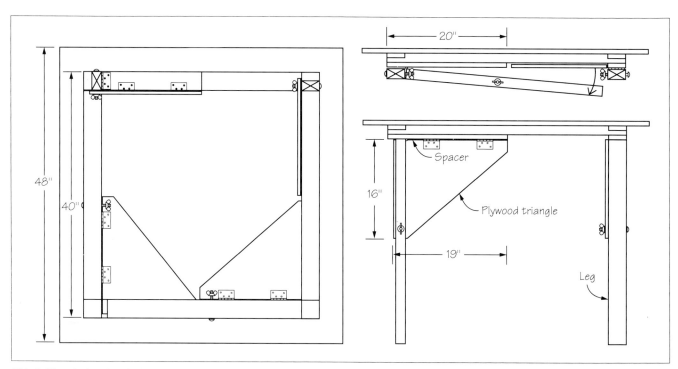

*This table mimics the old folding card table. Each leg is on a hinge and bolts to a folding plywood support.*

# 36 RADIAL ARM SAW BENCH

A radial arm saw is a very convenient but limited tool to have in your shop. Though it is possible to do a wide variety of jobs with a radial arm, such as ripping, sanding, even planing with a special head, you will find the tool difficult to use for these operations. The mechanical configuration of the machine makes it difficult to work accurately. But that same mechanical configuration renders the tool highly capable of cross cutting. For that reason, professional shops find the radial arm saw to be the tool of choice for cutting stock to length as well as cutting dadoes across boards of lesser width (depending on the length of the arm).

To make best use of this capability, you really need to mount the tool in a bench to support the other end of the board while it is cut. Because of this, a radial arm saw takes up a lot of room. If you don't have the room, you are probably better off doing your cross cutting on the table saw and making dadoes with a router. If you have the room, you can buy used radial arms relatively inexpensively, and you'll be very pleased with the convenience of being able to do quick and easy cutoffs.

The photo here shows a small radial arm saw mounted in a rather large bench setup made by my shopmate Tom Goode. He does professional cabinetry and so needs a large setup. Your setup, however, can be much smaller. Still, several things he did here are worth considering for your setup.

Why didn't he use a larger capacity machine? He didn't need it. Smaller capacity models (10" blades) will cut through 2" stock with only a little difficulty, and they will do fine on ¾" stock. Get a good quality carbide crosscut blade to make best use of your saw.

You don't have to make such a large bench around your saw. The large bench shown here is convenient for cutting down long boards, but you can do just fine building only an 8' bench to the left of your saw, and nothing to the right. Further, the cubbies beneath the bench are convenient for holding cutoff stock, but

*Mount your radial arm saw in a large bench against the wall like this, or build a smaller one to suit your needs.*

you may not need these and can support your bench with 2×4s angled from the bench edge to where the floor meets the wall.

Note the plywood cowling around the blade. This directs dust backward to a hole in the table, where it falls into a bucket for easy disposal. If you install a blower and ducting, consider running a line to your radial arm.

The hole shown in the bench top is for small cutoff pieces to be thrown into a large can, where they next go onto a pickup bed destined for the kindling box.

Lastly look at Tom Goode's smart cable arrangement on the top of the radial arm. These cables, attached to the wall, have turnbuckles that allow Tom to adjust the 90° cutoff angle very precisely, and then they hold it there steadily. Radial arm saws are notorious for losing adjustment, but this one stays firm. The drawback to using these cables is, of course, that they must be removed for angled cuts or raising the blade, then reinstalled and readjusted later.

# 37 FOLDING SAWHORSES

**Set up folding sawhorses when a bench isn't handy.**

Sawhorses are very handy for dealing with materials away from your bench, or dealing with materials that are too large for your bench. They are also bulky and cumbersome to store, unless they can fold like these horses, which take up minimal space.

Make these horses out of cheap framing 2×4 stock. But look through the stock at the yard carefully to find pieces that are relatively straight, free of sap, and have a minimum of knots. Knots are really only a problem on this project when they are located at the joints where you will bore for dowels. Boring through knots is, well, not what you want to do. Though most framing lumber is supposedly "kiln dried," don't be too surprised to find wet lumber. Wet pieces will be

noticeably heavier than the others. Pick lighter pieces in the hopes that they are fairly dry, because glue will not hold in wet lumber.

For a pair of sawhorses, buy two 12' studs and one 8'. Before you cut out the pieces, mark out on all three studs exactly where each piece will come from, and arrange your cutting pattern so that there are "not knots" where the "dowels do." The 8' stud gives you about 2' extra stock so you have some leeway in where you make your cuts. From this, cut out four pieces at 36", four at 32½", and two at 29". The four 36" pieces constitute the two top pieces and the two swinging legs. The 32½" pieces are the legs, and

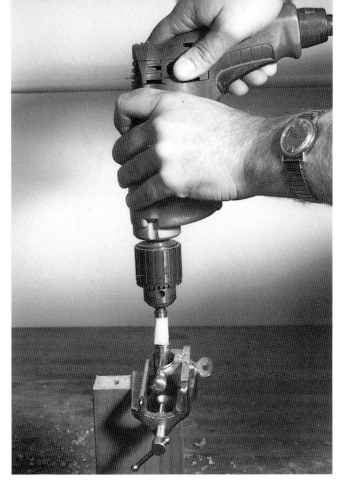

Photo 1—Bore the parts for ½" dowels using a doweling jig.

Photo 2—Bore rope holes in the lower cross rails and swinging legs, and install a length of rope that will keep the legs from swinging too far.

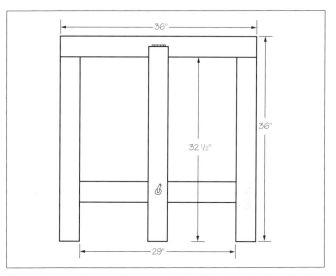

Make the parts for your horses out of 2×4 framing lumber. Avoid heavy, wet wood because glue won't adhere to it.

the 29" pieces are the lower cross rails.

The length of the lower cross rails must equal the length of the top pieces minus twice the width of the legs. The width of the legs, however, will probably vary so you must make the exact length of the cross rails to suit your actual pieces.

Bore the parts for ½" dowels with a doweling jig as shown in photo 1. Space the dowels about 1½" apart, centered on the ends of the legs and lower cross piece. Place the lower cross piece about 8" above the bottom of the legs.

Don't alter the design of the horses. You want the legs to come full height and the top piece to fit between the legs. Leave the top cross piece on top of the legs, so that downward force is transferred from the top piece to the legs, and not via the dowels. This way you are only depending on the dowels to keep the parts aligned, and not to support weight on the horses.

Buy a pair of light-duty 3½" interior door hinges to connect the swinging legs to the top pieces. Cut the swinging legs about ½" shorter than the total height of the glued frames. Lay the swinging legs onto their respective frames, and align the bottom of all three legs. This shows you where to place the hinge at the top. Making the swinging leg a bit shorter guarantees that it will be lower than the top edge of the horse,

and won't interfere with what's sitting on top. Attach the swinging legs to the top pieces with the hinges.

Bore holes in the swinging leg and lower cross rail for rope that will hold the legs, preventing them from swinging too far. See the photo 2. Cut the rope and tie knots so the leg is a little over 1' from the lower cross rails. If you were careful about how you cut out the lower cross rails, the rope holes in them will be such that the rope knots are not close to knots (pun intended).

# 38 ROLLER STAND

This little helper comes in handy whenever you need to guide long stock into or out of a machine. This design is simple and quick to make, using mostly screws for joinery, and is strong enough for light-duty tasks. If you want a heavier duty model, use this basic design with 2×4 framing lumber, and make the three joints of the upper T arm with mortises and tenons.

Get out all your parts from ¾"-thick stock as shown on the list. Set up a ¾" dado in the table saw, along with your miter gauge and a support fence as shown in photo 1 (page 129). Use this to cut slots in both the longer and shorter base pieces. Adjust the width of the dado with paper shims so that it matches the thickness of the stock. The two grooves should

***Use a roller stand to support long work coming into or going out of any machine.***

interlock for a tight joint as shown. Place one screw up from below in the outer foot to secure the joint.

The two center pieces of the upper T must be spaced apart an adequate distance for the carriage bolts that fit between them. Use the bolts as spacers to position these pieces when they are clamped for screwing as in photo 2 (page 129).

You must have the roller you intend to use for the stand in hand when you build the upper T to support it so that you will know exactly what dimensions to use. (See supplier's list for rollers.) Bore holes in the end supports for the roller pin, set the height of these

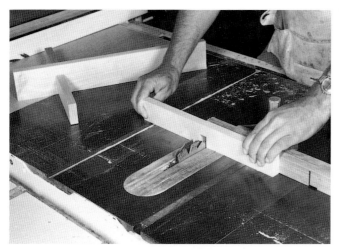

*Photo 1—Cut mating slots in the basic pieces so they join by interlocking. Setup with a dado and miter guage as shown.*

*Photo 2—Space the two center pieces for the upper T with the carriage bolts that will go between them. Screw them together with the short connector as shown.*

## MATERIALS LIST

| Part | | Dimension |
|------|---|-----------|
| A | Vertical base riser | ¾" × 3" × 26" |
| B | Horizontal base piece | ¾" × 3" × 20" |
| C | Horizontal base pieces (2) | ¾" × 2" × 12" |
| D | T center pieces (2) | ¾" × 1⁵⁄₁₆" × 26" |
| E | Horizontal T, length | ¾" × 3" × * |

*This measurement is determined by the size of your roller. Cut vertical roller holders and short connector for center pieces from scrap.

pieces just below the top of the roller so they won't interfere with work passing across the top.

Glue and screw the center base piece to the foot assembly, and screw the side slides to it. Glue and screw the center pieces of the upper T assembly to the top cross piece, again using the carriage bolts for spacers. Install the carriage bolts with wing nuts and you're ready to go.

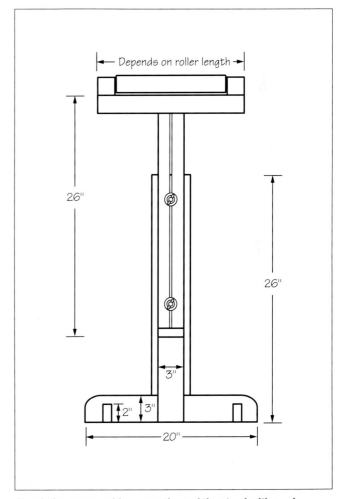

*Attach the upper and lower sections of the stand with carriage bolts and wing nuts.*

# 39 PLANNING FOR PROJECTS

**W**hat do I do first?" was the rather baffling question I asked myself when I began building furniture years ago. I made a few mistakes with my beginning projects, such as not coming up with a complete design at the start, which resulted in my tearing apart a project because parts didn't fit correctly. Another example of my stunning brilliance was discovering, after cutting out the parts, that if I had planned how to cut them out more carefully, I would have wasted less wood and had fewer short and useless cutoffs left over.

These examples point to the most important aspect of taking on any project—planning. It takes time at the beginning of any project to sit and figure out what you are going to do, and the temptation is always to just jump right in. But you will save yourself headaches and frustration later by knowing beforehand what you will be doing at each step in the process. I leave myself some flexibility here, because unanticipated problems may necessitate a small change in design or use of different joinery. But carefully planning the major structural aspects and joinery choices of a project before touching wood makes for a smoother procedure overall with far fewer mishaps.

## Using Printed Plans

Buying books, magazines and project plans reduces the amount of time you have to spend planning and developing your own design. But don't assume that you have to follow those plans exactly. Maybe you want your project to have slightly or very different dimensions than those shown on the page. Perhaps you don't have the tooling or confidence to do some of the joinery called for by the author. Go ahead and make the necessary changes to suit your desired dimensions, or tooling and skills capabilities. Don't pass up a project just because it doesn't quite meet your needs as is.

When you do make changes, you need to study the entire plan to see how these changes affect any and all other parts. This may seem like a daunting task, but you should look over a complete set of plans to see how all the parts fit before you start, regardless of whether you plan to make changes. This is partly because there is the possibility that the author made a mistake on the drawing (yes, we're human), but it's also to guarantee that you understand what it is you are about to make. This will help tremendously if you run across a problem that isn't dealt with in the plans. You will simply be more confident with the overall project knowing how all the parts fit together to make a whole.

When you consider joinery alternatives, it's a good idea to make drawings of some of the joints to ensure that you place various parts of the new joint in locations that don't conflict with other parts. Your new joinery may or may not cause the dimensions of the parts joined to change; it could also cause the dimensions of other parts to change. Drawings will show you this and give you a reference to use as you make and fit the parts.

## Design Your Own Projects

Does making your own design seem like an impossible task? It's not—if you plan carefully—and it lets you custom design your furniture to the way you want it, rather than having to settle for a printed plan that's *almost* what you want. Here's a step-by-step process for designing your own project.

One—determine the overall dimensions. Come up with a height, width and depth according to your needs. Find a similar piece in an antique shop and use its dimensions.

Two—choose construction type. Frame and panel construction? Solid slabs? Plywood? Decide what you want according to your desires as well as your tooling capabilities and skills. Look at other project plans for general construction and joinery ideas.

Three—get specific with joinery. Look at all parts of the project, and see how you will join the pieces to each other. Choose designs that avoid cross-grain conflict from moisture variations, and choose joinery that will be strong enough for the task.

Four—flesh it out. Make an exact scale drawing of the project with front, side and top views. Make other section views as necessary to show how internal parts fit. Fill in all the internal dimensions, and add them all up to be certain that they match the external dimensions. This is one of your best self-checking devices.

Whether you are working from printed plans or your own plans, don't feel compelled to stick exactly to what's on paper. Aside from problems that arise that necessitate change, you simply might want to make a change because it looks like it will be better to you as you are making the parts. The problem here is that if you make too many changes, you affect a lot of your original plan and you have to rework it, making it seem useless. But without any plan, you have nothing to refer to for your major dimensions, so you don't know what your changes will affect. I develop my plans through far enough so that I know the major design and construction aspects are covered. I come up with a tentative plan for smaller details, and either use it or not, depending on what I think at the time. One way or the other, I have a larger structure within which to fit or refit any changes.

## If All Else Fails, Read the Instructions

That bit of humorous wisdom applies when you are figuring out how to use your microwave oven, but not when you are following printed furniture plans. You should read instructions thoroughly before you start a project to understand how the whole is put together, and read them as you construct the project for specifics, but don't limit yourself to only what is included in those instructions. You might have a better way of accomplishing the very same procedure, or you might not have the tool described and need to use another. But, once again, carefully investigate how any changes you make might affect other parts.

## Cutting Out Your Parts

Once you are satisfied that you know the project well enough to begin, make up a cutout list and look at your stock. If you do not yet have stock, look at the list to find combinations of parts that fit well together in lengths you are most likely to find at the lumber yard, like 8', 10' and 12' pieces. But since hardwoods often come in random widths and lengths, this can be difficult. Make a rough drawing on paper with your parts, organizing them together in one long, wide board, and calculate how many board feet this theoretical board amounts to. A board foot is a unit of volume, 1' square and 1" (¾" finished) thick.

When you buy lumber, buy that number of board feet plus 20 percent. If you have a minimum of parts and you know there will be little waste, reduce that to 10 percent. If you have a lot of different-sized parts, and the stock you are picking through has a lot of defects, increase the percentage appropriately. Have your list with you and look for pieces that will most efficiently give you the largest parts for your project. The small parts will be easy to get from cutoff after you get your largest parts, but ensuring that you can get the large parts from relatively straight sections is most important.

Ultimately you will be able to use your stock most efficiently if you can choose your parts from a large number of sticks. If you can afford it, buy four times as much lumber as you need for the project (or just enough to get a price break), and keep the rest for future projects.

Always begin getting out your stock by accounting for your largest parts. Try to get your largest parts from the smallest pieces of rough stock you have. If you can do this, then your larger pieces of stock will be what you get the small parts from, and you can very efficiently use a large stick to cut out small parts. Also, if you always get your parts from the smallest available sticks, what is left over after you have cut out your parts is the largest stick you had. This stick will be more useful for other projects than the same amount of lumber in two or three shorter pieces.

As you are looking for the best board to get your largest parts from, look carefully at what you can do with what is cut off after the large pieces are taken. Using your smallest sticks for the largest parts is not the best idea when the cutoff that remains is too short to be useful, but large enough to be very wasteful. You may need to use your largest sticks to cut out your large parts simply because the combination of parts you can get with the cutoff works out best.

Ideally, you will find combinations of large and short parts that fit perfectly within your existing stock. In reality, you won't be so lucky, so find a combination that leaves a minimum of short waste. And, beware of end splits on all lumber. You might find a perfect combination of parts that uses all the length of the stick, only to find later that there was a 6" end split in the stick, which is now in your part. Mark end splits with chalk and cut them off.

# 40 WOOD STORAGE

f you build wooden storage racks against the wall for holding lumber, you will need to install triangular supports beneath the racks to hold them. These triangular supports reduce the available space beneath the rack. The solution is to use heavy 7-gauge steel beam brackets, firmly bolted to the wall.

Bore holes in sections of construction grade 4×4 timbers for lag screws to secure the timbers to the studs in your wall. Also bore the 4×4s for the L brackets. Locate one lag screw above and one below the upper bolt hole for each bracket. This will support the wood around these holes, which will take a lot of the load. Use large fender washers on the lags to hold the wood.

You must ensure that the lags are securely screwed into the wall studs, or disaster could result. Use a nail and hammer to punch holes in the wall board to locate the studs. Bore holes in the studs at the diameter of the lag shank behind the threads. Use lags long enough to go into the studs at least 2". When you torque them down, be sure they firm up solidly. If not, you missed the stud, or you hit a large crack in it and the lag is not doing anything. In this case, start over and relocate the racks.

Don't overload your racks. As a general rule of thumb, don't place over 1' high of lumber on the racks. But even this could be too much if your stock is very long. If in doubt, install a third or fourth set of racks for more support.

**Hold wood up on the wall to get it out of the way with these wood and steel racks.**

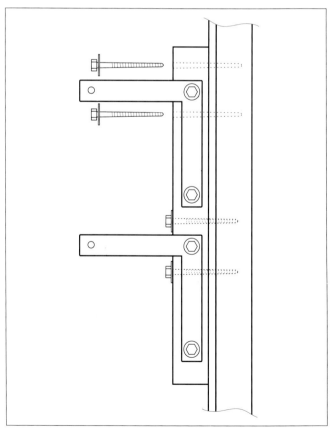

**Locate lag screws through the 4×4 supports and into wall studs. Place lags above and below the upper bolt for each steel L bracket.**

# LIST OF SUPPLIERS

Adjustable Clamp Co.
417 N. Ashland Ave.
Chicago IL 60622
(312) 666-0640
Press screws, as well as many other woodworking clamps.

AMT Co.
Box 70
Royersford PA 19468
(215) 948-0400
Dovetail jig, screwboxes, as well as many other woodworking tools.

Arco Products Corp.
110 W. Sheffield Ave.
Englewood NJ 07631
Dowel jig.

Delta Machinery
246 Alpha Dr.
Pittsburgh PA 15238
(412) 963-2400
Dust collectors and a book about same, as well as many woodworking machines and accessories.

De-Sta-Co
Box 2800
Troy MI 48007
(313) 589-2008
Wide assortment of toggle clamps.

Grizzly Imports
Box 2069
Bellingham WA 98227
(206) 647-0801
Dust collectors and a book about the same, as well as many woodworking machines and accessories.

Jet Equipment and Tools
Box 1477
Tacoma WA 98401
(206) 572-5000
Dust collectors and a book about the same, as well as many woodworking machines and accessories.

Jointech Corp.
Box 790727
San Antonio TX 78279
Dowel Crafter dowel jig and other woodworking jigs.

Keller and Co.
1327 I St.
Petaluma CA 94952
(707) 763-9336
Dovetail jig

Leichtung Workshops
4944 Commerce Parkway
Cleveland OH 44128
(800) 321-6840
Jointmaster dovetail, mortise and tenon, and finger joint jig, Universal tenoning jigs, dowel jigs, honing guide, handscrew kits, as well as many other woodworking tools.

Leigh Industries
Box 357
Port Coquitlam, British Columbia
Canada V3C 4K6
(604) 464-2700
Dovetail jigs and accessories.

Millercraft Inc.
Box 5586
Derwood MD 20855
Dovemaster dovetail jig.

Penn State Industries
2850 Comly Rd.
Philadelphia PA 91954
(800) 377-7297
Roller for roller stand, as well as numerous other woodworking tools and accessories.

Porter Cable
Box 2468
Jackson TN 38302
(901) 668-8600
Omnijig dovetailing fixture, another dovetail jig, routers and accessories.

Record Tools
1915 Clements Rd., #1
Pickering, Ontario
Canada L1W 3V1
(416) 428-1077
Steel vises, dowel jig, bench holdfasts, as well as many other woodworking tools.

Stanley Tools
Division of the Stanley Works
New Britain CT 06050
(203) 225-5111
Dowel jig, as well as many other woodworking tools.

Tool Aid
6950 Eric Ln.
Wheatland CA 95692
Rig A Mortise router mortising jig.

Vermont American
Box 340
Lincolnton NC 28092
Dovetail jig.

Wolfcraft
1222 W. Ardmore Ave.
Itasca IL 60143
(708) 773-4777
Dovetail jig.

Woodcraft
PO Box 1686
Parkersburg WV 26102-1686
(800) 225-1153
Bench holdfasts, bench dogs, Dowl-it jig, dowel points, screwboxes, steel bench screws, Porter Cable mortise and tenon jig, Bryco table saw tenoner, three honing guides, grinding wheel mandrel and wheels, shelf pins, as well as many other woodworking tools.

# INDEX